ISBN 978-1-952520-01-3 eBook / 978-1-952520-04-4 Paperback

Copyright ©2020 Tom Durwood

Cover illustration copyright ©2020 Zelda Devon

This work is dedicated to my cadets, whose ideas helped shape it, and to my two wonderful kids, whose coming-of-age stories are just unfolding.

Contents

Foreword II
Author's Welcome V
Introduction 7
Overview: A Brief History 9

PART ONE: YOUR LIT CRIT TOOLBOX

The Coming-of-Age Matrix 19
Identity and the Other 26
The Building Blocks of Literature 30
Gender 34
The Three-Act Structure 38
Class and Trauma 41
Billy Wilder's Rules 45
Images of War in Children's Literature 48
Empire 52

PART TWO: IN DEPTH STUDIES

The Lion King and Its Message of Social Darwinism 59
Star Wars and Government 69
How We See 'The Other' in *Tintin* 79
Imperialism in the "Tarzan" Franchise 90
Empire and Higher Education in Nnedi Okorafor's *Binti* 98
Phillip Pullman, Polar Bears and the Real Arctic ... 108
Pixar Gender, Pixar Rules 120
Philosophy in Comics 129
Harry Potter: Last of the Breed 137
A Revolution in Picture Books 148

PART THREE: LESSON PLANS

Nine Things to Know About Prof. Durwood's EN 210 Class 160
Our Mission 163
Index 200

Foreword

by Todd Whitaker

It is a pleasure to write the foreword for this book. My years as a teacher, principal and professor in educational leadership have continually reinforced the importance of literacy. To be a good reader we have to be a good thinker, and this book combines the two very well.

There are twin premises to Tom Durwood's "Kid Lit: An Introduction to Literary Criticism." The first is that literary theory is for all of us, and the second is that students can develop marketable lifetime skills when building critical thinking regarding their favorite stories.

Tom is a teacher and it is quickly evident in the clarity of his writing. He poses a simple question – for example, *What makes a good villain?* -- and then draws you into a comparison between Captain Ahab (apocalyptic evil) and Dr. Octopus (simple greed). This then flows into a consideration of evil in all literature. You are then invited to formulate your own theory of good and bad by following his clear illustrations.

This is a unique book in that the three sections are quite different. Part One is the 'critical tool box' and begins with the elements of the universal coming-of-age narrative. The author then shows young readers and general readers how to recognize story structure, class, gender, symbolism, trauma and Orientalism in children's narratives. His consideration is broad and inclusive. We meet many recurring literary characters that will challenge historical stereotypes.

The second section of "Kid Lit: An Introduction to Literary Criticism" is a sampling of new scholarship in children's literature. Tom introduces and then interviews rising scholars like Amanda Lagji, Alexander Maxwell and Anna Kozak. Readers will discover:

… a breakdown of Afrofuturism and other schools of the 'Empire Writes Back' movement

… why scholars of the family consider *Finding Nemo* a step forward and *The Incredibles* a step backward

… the vital connection between *Star Wars* and Vietnam

… the social Darwinian structure supporting the animal monarchy of *The Lion King*

… why *Kung Fu Panda* and *The Hobbit* are the same story, just as *Avatar* and *Dances with Wolves* are the same movie

Part Three is the fun and immediately practical part, especially for teachers, where we see just how to bring these concepts into the classroom. The 28 pages of ready-to-implement lessons in the book's third section give readers a taste of what it's like to spend a semester in Tom's class. These lesson plans are the proof of the pudding: every teacher needs classroom activities and exercises that allow students to apply their learning to their own lives. Here, the underlying dynamics of *Harry Potter* and *The Secret Garden* and *The Hunger Games* render lessons in gender, race, trauma, identity and the Other. Tom wants students to connect these elements to their own coming-of-age narratives.

This book is not a typical read and may not be for everyone. To those looking for a linear dissertation connecting *Peter Rabbit* to Michel Foucault and post-structuralism, it will seem disjointed. "Kid Lit: An Introduction to Literary Criticism" is a collection of ideas, and what it lacks in continuity it makes up for in robustness. This is literary criticism at its least formal and most lively. It will definitely challenge you and your students thinking. It will also energize you on ways to apply these practices to other readings you use in your classroom.

This is also a book on a mission, which is (in Tom's words):

> "*Wake up!* Stop being passive consumers of these narratives. You must begin to own these stories, break them down and see what makes them tick. It will lead to a life of critical thinking, which is beyond value."

Children's literature is a vibrant field, always growing and changing. There is plenty of room for new approaches like this one. What comes through the pages of "Kid Lit" is an authentic love of literature. Readers and teachers alike will find in it a useful and worthwhile resource. Get ready to dive in and enjoy a new perspective to literature.

-- Todd Whitaker
August, 2020

Todd Whitaker is a professor of educational leadership at Indiana State University in Terre Haute, Indiana. He is a leading presenter in the field of education and has written more than 40 books, including the national bestseller, *What Great Teachers Do Differently*.

He regularly presents at conferences such as the National Association of Secondary School Principals (NASSP), the Association for Supervision and Curriculum Development (ASCD), the Academy of Management Learning and Education, and the National Association of Elementary School Principals (NAESP).

Author's Welcome

In my classroom, students enjoy using critical theory on literature.

If I can present Lit Crit in a way they can understand, my students relish the opportunity to give their analysis of Nigel Longbottom, or The Vision's android love for the Scarlet Witch, or the Omega Knights and their doomed manga brethren who patrol dystopian worlds (always with swords).

This collection started as a file of material from my Empire and Literature course. In the first part, I outline some of the basic tools we use in literary analysis. In the second part, I present six case studies, in which young scholars tackle specific Kid Lit topics. In the third part, I list resources which should be useful for all readers.

Fellow teachers and general readers, you should take what you like. Fashion your own lesson plans. I hope you disagree with my ideas!

To answer the question that all students are now asking, even if they are polite enough not to say it out loud: Who cares about all this?

Well, you do. Young readers must begin taking control of their worlds, starting with becoming an active reader. Learn and own the conventions of all those stories you passively consume. Look under the hood. Think critically, in all things. This is just the beginning.

The other portion of this book is online. You will find links to the online postings of the full original text of the Section Two authors' work – representing another 60 pages of original Kid Lit scholarship.

You also have free access to a collection of lesson plans for the "Kid Lit" material – another 40 pages of associated content. Much of this has been adapted to an interactive format by an excellent educator named Josilyn Markel. Here is the link:

www.kidlitcrit.com/teacher-resource/

Your fellow reader,
Tom Durwood

Kid Lit

AN INTRODUCTION TO LITERARY CRITICISM

Maxfield Parrish "Arabian Nights" (1908)

Introduction

Wikimedia Commons

Children's literature should be subjected to critical rigour as much as grown-up writing … Children's literature occupies a very different position from literature as a whole, largely because of two things: it's part of nurturing, in the anthropological sense, but it's also part of education.

-- Michael Rosen, The Independent

Behind any child's book or theory of children's literature is a view of children and their upbringing.

-- Michael Prest, "Why it Pays to Study Children's Literature"

Our mission in this book, yours and mine, is to answer this simple question: *What makes for children's literature that endures?*

Whether we like *Tintin* or *Gears of War* or not, there is a secret to these stories' incredible appeal. We need to understand that appeal, on its surface as well in its deeper meanings. Millions of young readers devotedly consume these narratives, decade after decade. *Why? What makes the story tick? What are the ideas beneath its surface?*

The answer surely lies in filling a need, or filling a developmental need among our young readers, or matching a societal imperative. Let's find out. There are no correct answers, nor is there any single way to approach such critical thinking.

> **Your teachers want you to think for yourself, to analyze why things happen, to look under the hood. So will all of your bosses.**

For students, teachers, and readers of all narratives: we must each develop our own theory of literature. **We are defined by narratives**, in our politicians, our schools, our workplaces. Each family has defining coming-of-age stories, and love stories, and success stories. What elements are authentic about these stories? What structures are 'borrowed'? How are they connected? What are the conventions of each genre of story?

Your teachers and I do not want you to agree with the viewpoints in this book: **we want you to form your own theory**. Why are these superhero stories good? Why are they bad? What is the measure of a good story well told? State and justify your theory. Construct an argument. Assemble a chain of logic. Give specific examples. Be clear.

Your teachers want you to think for yourself, to analyze why things happen, to look under the hood. So will all of your bosses. Critical thinking and clear expression are highly marketable skills.

> **You do not have to buy what I'm selling. It's worse: you have to understand it, break it down, reply to it, and then produce your own theory to replace mine.**

OVERVIEW
A Brief History

In this book, we take a deliberately broad and inclusive approach to the field of Children's Literature (Kid Lit).

Any definition of Kid Lit would start with picture books for toddlers, primary-colored books aimed at building fundamental reading and spelling skills. Then simple stories are introduced in picture books to develop an understanding of language and to provide basic information about the world – what a giraffe is, how giraffes compare to cows, where carrots and trains come from, socks and shoes, where the moon lives, etc. As young readers approach the teen years, they graduate to **chapter books** which present a longer narrative in segments. These can be myths, legends, folk tales, and a broad spectrum of fiction – realistic, contemporary, fantasy, historical, teen romance. A librarian might also include non-fiction or informational books, biographies, poetry and drama in the children's literature section. Films are literature, so the current boom of young-adult and superhero narratives on our screens is fair game. At the upper margins of Kid Lit are sophisticated coming-of-age stories like *To Kill a Mockingbird* and *Catcher in the Rye*.

Here is my crude overview of four historic phases of children's literature. The scholarly works listed after my overview will give you a more refined history of a genre that has only recently captured scholars' attention.

ONE: FOLK AND FAIRY TALES MAKE IT INTO PRINT

Starting with the first stories told around a campfire, centuries of oral tradition produced a voluminous body of folk tales. Once the Gutenberg revolution of printed books took hold in the 17th century, these little morality plays were recorded. It was the German Grimm Brothers, Wilhelm and Jacob, who compiled the earliest blockbuster collection of folk tales in the early 19th century, a generation after the first alphabet book. The Brothers Grimm changed the tales as they recorded them, as had every storyteller before them. *Snow White, The Pied Piper, Hansel and Gretel, the Musicians of Bremen* and *Rumpelstiltskin* are just a few of the two hundred tales retold by the Grimms.

Frenchman Charles Perrault preceded the Grimms with a collection of French fairy tales, and the Italian Carlo Colladi's Pinocchio followed them. Sir Richard Burton contributed a colorful volume of Arabian tales, *Arabian Nights Entertainments, Or The Book of a Thousand Nights and a Night,* which reflected English dreams of the Orient more than any reality of the Orient.

> **Ever since Bruno Bettelheim wrote "The Uses of Enchantment" about the psychological meaning of fairy tales, child psychologists have looked at storytelling as an important tool children use to work through their anxieties about the adult world.**
>
> **Fairy-tale fantasies are now regarded as almost literal depictions of childhood fears about abandonment, powerlessness, and death.**
>
> -- Colleen Gillard

TWO: A CROP OF BRITISH CLASSICS

As the modern age dawned at the end of the 19th century, a brief yet remarkable cultural moment produced stories brimming with self-confidence, stories we now call Children's Classics. These include the two book which set the standard for all coming-of-age (COA) adventures to follow, Robert Louis Stevenson's *Treasure Island* and *Kidnapped*; J.M. Barrie's *Peter Pan*; Lewis Carroll's *Alice in Wonderland* and *Through the Looking Glass*; Rudyard Kipling's *The Jungle Book* and *Just So Stories*; Kenneth Grahame's *The Wind in the Willows*; and A.A. Milne's *Winnie the Pooh* (in the Golden Age's later phase), Beatrix Potter's *Peter Rabbit* books, Hugh Lofting's *Doctor Doolittle*, and more. Each is infused with a sort of storytelling bravado, original characters in vivid settings, with storytelling and language of the highest order. These are stories celebrating Britishness, taking place in worlds complete with imperial comforts and class systems. They reflect a culture of unprecedented self-confidence, produced by a moment of imperial bravado. The words were matched by images from illustrators like Arthur Rackham, Edmund Dulac, Ernest Shepherd and Americans Howard Pyle and N.C. Wyeth. These 'classics' made a permanent stamp on children's imaginations, and dominated the next half-century of children's literature.

N.C. Wyeth

THREE: THE EXPLOSION OF MODERN KID LIT

After World War I, everything changed. The romantic, naïve stories of the British-driven Golden Age were no longer valid in the modern century, not after machine-driven warfare had obliterated an entire generation of Englishmen. Idyllic gardens and bunny capers gave way to a far less insular and certain view of the world. New styles of narration, one more tied to modern reality, emerged, and along with it a mid-century rebirth of children's literature. In a relatively brief time – between 1925 and 1975 – modern children's literature blossomed.

American virtues rose. Children's stories like *Little Orphan Annie*, Frank Baum's *Oz* series and Laura Ingalls Wilder's *Little House on the Prairie* reflected an American sensibility. Colleen Gillard, writing in *The Atlantic*, points out that American stories "are more notable for their realistic portraits of day-to-day life in the towns and farmlands on the growing frontier … Americans are defined by a Protestant work ethic that can still be heard in stories like *Pollyanna* or *The Little Engine That Could*."

In the late 1930's, enter a one-man revolution in early reader books. **Dr. Seuss**'s injected fun, surprise and fresh wordplay in books like *Horton Hears A Who* and *The Cat in the Hat*. Advances in graphics and printing provided the platform for a new generation of illustrators influenced by abstract art and blocks of color to expand the Kid Lit visual universe -- captivating artists like of Maurice Sendak, Eric Carle Peter Sis (to name three). Subjects like death (*I Miss My Grandpa*, by Jin Xiaojing), divorce (*Dear Mr. Henshaw*, by Beverly Cleary) and nuclear war *Sadako and the Thousand Paper Cranes* were no longer off-limits. Books like Susanna Kaysen's *Girl, Interrupted* began to deal with depression and mental illness among young adults. Outcast kids (*Diary of a Wimpy Kid*) could now be celebrated.

Thoughtful and not-always-upbeat books like Shel Silverstein's *The Giving Tree* and the elegiac *The Little Prince* by Antoine de Saint-Exupery appeared alongside European picture-book adventures of characters like Asterix, Babar,

Curious George and Tintin, which explored the cultural encounters of a newly global modern world.

A similar broadening process occurred in the Kid Lit depiction of family life. The traditional representation of the family in children's works never strayed far from the model of the "nuclear family," with a father working outside the home, a mother attending children and housework, and happy children at home. This idealized depiction of familial life began to diversify in the 1960s. Authors like Beverly Cleary, Judy Blume and S.E Hinton portrayed a wider spectrum of family life. Children's literature reached for more complex issues, portraying new and challenging family situations. Protagonists with rich and sometimes anguished inner lives dealt with in books like *Heather Has Two Mommies* (1989) by Lesléa Newman, and Becky Albertalli's *Simon vs the Homo Sapiens Agenda*.

Beginning with *Steamboat Willie* in 1928, **Walt Disney and the Disney Studio** (and subsequent multi-media empire, which now includes Pixar) became the most voluminous single global storytelling generator of modern times. Disney characters and values have heavily impacted five generations of children. Scholars have written scores of books and hundreds of articles analyzing the messages within the Disney body of work.

One of the most influential single children's literary property in this era was J.R.R. Tolkien's *Lord of the Rings* trilogy (along with the companion book, *The Hobbit*). What began as an experiment in medieval linguistics became an elvish epic which spawned an entire genre of epic fantasies, among them *Game of Thrones*.

The first appearance of the great COA story, Tarzan (1912)

FOUR: THE CURRENT GOLDEN AGE

The 21st century has brought a new golden age for children's literature. As technology has expanded, so have coming-of-age stories proliferated and expanded in form and content.

Led by Marvel, *Star Wars*, *Harry Potter* and social games, children's literature now rules the media. Comic books have taken over mainstream media: in 2019, four of the ten top-grossing films are comic-book derived. A one-woman literary movement of her own, J.K. Rowling's impact on Kid Lit is seismic, comparable to that of Dr. Seuss.

GAMING AS LITERATURE

With the advent of computer-based reproduction techniques, the process of full color reproduction has been revolutionized. Now almost any story or set of pictures can be conveyed in multiple platforms.

Online gaming, social gaming and video gaming constitute a new, dazzling hybrid form of interactive storytelling. The collective popularity of games (forecast to reach $230 billion in global revenues by 2022) dwarfing other media. These open-ended adventures feature mysteries, role-playing, battle as well as dozens of ingenious premises and original characters. The dazzling visuals create fictional worlds that go far beyond a printed page.

Vanderbilt University's course, "Online Games: Literature, New Media and Narrative" demonstrates the breadth of this new generation of storytelling. "Games mimic life: things happen which are unexpected, there are challenges, we make mistakes," argues Dr. Alistair Brown of Durham University. "At the same time, these mistakes and backward paths are more enjoyable in the context of a game because we know that they must lead somewhere."

NEW AND MULTICULTURAL PERSPECTIVES

Authors like Virginia Hamilton, Mildred Taylor, Alma Flor Ada, and Walter Dean Myers are bringing 'buried' narratives to the surface – the untold stories of the 'conquered.' *Pemmican Wars: A Girl Called Echo* by Katherena Vermette and the anthology *Not Your Princess* tell us about Native American lives. The picture book *W is For Wombat* by Aboriginal artist Bronwyn Bancroft gives us all a window into Aboriginal culture. A growing collection of titles like Jacqueline Woodson's *Brown Girl Dreaming* and Kwame Alexander's Newberry Medal-winning *The Crossover* reflect the difficult rise of African Americans. Chinese American author Grace Lin's *Where the Mountain Meets the Moon* tells the tale of an Asian family. Manga, a different and often sophisticated sub-genre of comic books, are hugely popular in Japan.

The Binti books by Okorafor and Tomi Adeyemi's *Children of Blood and Bone* represent a new wave of authors whose works form a sort of reply to J.R.R. Tolkien – these are epic fantasies written from diverse cultural perspectives, in this case an African perspective. *Afrofuturism* is a term coined for the marriage of technology and black diaspora culture, a vibrant and growing niche within children's literature.

There is still a long way to go to represent all cultures fairly. As Dashka Slater, writing in *Mother Jones*, notes, "when the Cooperative Children's Book Center at the University of Wisconsin-Madison looked at 3,200 children's books published in the United States last year, it found that only 14 percent had black, Latino, Asian, or Native American main characters."

Wikimedia Commons

PART ONE
Your Lit Crit Toolbox

Edmund Dulac's "The Snow Queen" (1911)

Note from Tom

In this opening section you will find brief introductions to basic ideas that smart readers want to carry in their critical tool kits.

These conceptual instruments will help you to unlock a literary property, to answer the questions, 'Why is this story so enduring? What makes it tick?'

The tools are not interchangeable, and some will work better than others on any given story. Class theory, for example, sheds some light on a Kid Lit narrative like *A Secret Garden*, but gender is much more effective. Applying "Geography is Destiny" to *Sam I Am* yields almost nothing.

Your Sherpa,

Tom

CHAPTER ONE
The Coming-of-Age Matrix

Wikimedia Commons

This is the most useful section of my book.

This matrix or set of ideas is nothing new, rather a skeleton or structure for stories we have told from Day One. All cultures.

There are several different versions of it. Early (early to me, anyway) scholars who outlined the elements of the Coming of Age (COA) story include a German psychologist named Otto Rank, the great psychoanalyst Carl Jung, and Joseph Campbell, whose book "Hero with a Thousand Faces" has been so influential. A century earlier than Otto Rank, a German scholar named Karl Morgenstern listed the conventions of the "bildungsroman," or 'formation novel,' a specific form of the COA.

In the COA story, the young protagonist (hero or heroine) is initiated into adulthood through an adventure. The adventure introduces the hero to the adult world – a world in imbalance, full of tragedy, turmoil and disillusionment. The story's end is a resolution, leaving the world with a balancing of scales. The protagonist has journeyed from innocence to painful wisdom. Childhood is gone. With the hard-won wisdom from this quest, the protagonist can join the ranks of successful adults.

Here are the basic elements of the coming of age story:

a) beloved state of innocence at the story's beginning

b) foreshadowing = the hint that big change is about to come

c) knotty situation or moral dilemma developing

d) the central, tragic (often violent) event that marks the loss of innocence

e) call to action = the hero leaves home on a quest

f) gaining a sidekick

g) gaining a second name = the hero now belongs to two worlds

h) betrayer or villain

i) the innocent hero becomes the agent of change = the chosen one

j) wise older guide who shows the way forward

k) the unexpected gaining of advantage (magic trinket, weapon, etc.)

l) defeat of a minor villain

m) crucial encounters with nature – one good, one bad

n) revelation of the true nature of evil (it's worse than you thought)

o) betrayal and loss of close companion = a new low

p) one last chance appears in the dark hour …

q) moment of clarity = the hero's realization of his/her true potential

r) climactic battle with the forces of evil = act of retribution

s) harmony and justice return to the world

Please test these!! Make a chart with these elements on one axis and six children's stories on the second axis and see how many elements fit each story, and which diverges from the model. Some, like the first *Star Wars* trilogy and *The Hobbit*, check every single element.

Nonfiction The Coming-of-Age rules fit in the real world, as well as in fictional worlds. Homer Hickam's admirable *October Sky* is an autobiography that checks all of the COA boxes, as does a book like Saroo Brierley's *A Long Way Home*. One aspect of the narrative is often gets more attention – the science in *October Sky*, the epic journey in *A Long Way Home*, but they are still the same story.

The hero story often begins with **the hero's special birth** and **flawed or absent parent figures**. Something wrong in the hero's family tends to mirror the greater issue in the story's society – there is usually a violent or epic or dramatic social movement taking place in the background (war, civil rights, etc).

Other 'failed' grownup figures appear along the way, sad role models of children who did not successfully make a successful transition to adulthood.

The hero is usually a figure of two worlds, and is known by two names. Like you and me, she has a social name -- a name among her peers – and then a truer, private, forever name which refers to a secret heritage (and latent special powers).

The hero's encounter with nature is sometimes in the form of a divine intervention – an encounter with the supernatural.

One of N. C. Wyeth's illustrations for the COA classic "Treasure Island."

Sub-categories of sidekicks include the Jester (San Gamgee), **the Rebel** (Han Solo) and **the Innocent** (the Snowman in *Frozen*). Other recurring characters include **the Magic negro** (John Coffey in *The Green Mile*), who uses his powers to further the white savior's quest; **the noble savage**, often a foe-turned-friend; **the savage conquest** (a type of girlfriend, often the chieftain's daughter, as in *Avatar*); and Lotus Flower Woman, the lucky Asian female (the wife of Tom Cruise's fallen foe in *The Last Samurai*) who gets to bandage and enlighten the male hero.

Heroes often patrol a "borderland" -- a place outside civilized society, on the remote frontiers -- where they a) gain valuable information or b) fight their epic encounters with evil. It is often far away from friendly places with families, schools, warm light and stores. For example, modern-day heroes of the U.S. military patrol the "borderlands" or Afghanistan. Nicolas Cage in the motorcyclist-on-fire movie fought his demonic foes in a gigantic cemetery. Batman first encountered Ras-Al-Ghul in the far mountains of Tibet.

THE VILLAIN IS AS IMPORTANT TO THE STORY AS THE HERO

Villains and their motivations differ greatly. **Evil can be either human and social, or cosmic**. *The Terminator* movies feature apocalyptic evil, while a villain like Doctor Octopus in Spiderman represents one man's good intentions gone terribly bad. *Harry Potter* features both categories of villainy – Valdemort is apocalyptic evil, and the blockheaded Minister of Magic's villainy seems more rooted in his personal vanity. Terrorism is today often portrayed as apocalyptic – a cosmic force, something we cannot prevent or understand. Movies like *White House Down, Independence Day, Green Lantern,* and *War of the Worlds* feature evil like this – a force you cannot really understand (but must defeat). Certainly the Joker in *The Dark Knight* is like this -- he wants to bring general chaos to Gotham City for no rational reason. By contrast, the villain Bane in *The Dark Knight Rises* had a specific human story behind his villainy. Jack Torrance, the bad guy in Stephen King's *The Shining,* is an unlucky man controlled by a higher evil force.

American evil is often hedonism. Because of America's Puritanical streak, we tend to portray our villains as high-living creeps who transgress the work ethic. They are hedonistic – they enjoy material things way too much. They represent bad values. The *Die Hard* films, for example, feature villains who want to get ahead without working hard and playing by the rules – they want to cheat. That is why they are so despicable. Corporate villains (*Robocop*) often fall into this category.

Each villain may be simply the mirror image of its hero. Captain America is a strong smart hero (with no special powers) fighting for democracy, so the Red Skull is a strong smart Nazi (with no special powers) opposing him. That is why you can never switch villains – Lex Luthor does not fit against Luke Skywalker.

Henchmen are minor villains and may not need a theory at all.

In the hero's final battle with evil, **an ancestor often plays a key role**, providing a trinket or weapon or special motto of self-understanding. Uncovering the 'real' truth about one's past looms large in a successful quest.

My students always enjoy filling out (and arguing over) the coming-of-age matrix. As they enter the classroom, I am drawing on the chalkboard a giant chart listing some of the most common elements on the left. As soon as class starts, I ask for their favorite protagonists, fictional or real. We include a student or student's parent, since the coming of age saga applies to fictional characters and their readers alike. We list those names on the top line, and then we check off who fits the bill (they all do).

It's impossible to fill out the COA chart and then read a teen book or see a teen movie without connecting the two. This is the essence of Lit Crit – seeing patterns, overt and hidden, among stories.

A Sampling of Coming-of-Age Novels

To Kill a Mockingbird
Treasure Island, Kidnapped
Peter Pan
The Fault in Our Stars
Once and Future King / The Sword in the Stone
Boys in the Hood
Persepolis
The Twilight series
The Harry Potter series
A Tree Grows in Brooklyn
Lord of the Flies
Persepolis
Alice in Wonderland
The Color Purple

Any book by SE Hinton
The Autobiography of Malcolm X
Catcher in the Rye
Great Expectations
Huck Finn
The Red Badge of Courage
Island of the Blue Dolphins
All Quiet on the Western Front

A Sampling of Coming-of-Age Films

A Walk to Remember
Kung Fu Panda
Juno
October Sky
Carrie
Star Wars #1
Harry Potter series
Twilight (any)
Diner
Any Disney Movie
Forrest Gump
American Graffiti
Good Will Hunting
My Girl
Stand By Me
West Side Story
Breaking Away
How to Train Your Dragon
The Karate Kid

CHAPTER TWO
Identity and the Other

Wikimedia Commons

I am safe in saying that identity is a theme in a majority of children's literature. This is an umbrella term and can include anything from family lineage to gender to personal destiny. Protagonists in children's literature usually move from innocence to hard-won wisdom, and in the last chapter, they are more who they were meant to be. By story's end, protagonists like Mowgli, Pippi Longstocking, and Po the Kung Fu Panda have all claimed their true identities.

There is also such a thing as a national identity story. Scholars like me like to point out that Daniel Boone and Little Orphan Annie are American figures in the Kid Lit landscape, individualists who fight for their own place in the world, and could never be produced by an Inuit culture (for instance), a culture that values the group over the individual. A most excellent writer named Evan Osnos believes the Chinese national narrative has to do with a fear of being overrun by foreigners. "National humiliation is not a new idea in China," he offers.

Anne of Green Gables is cited as a cornerstone in the construction of a Canadian identity by scholars like York University's Danielle Russell. Anne is an orphan who struggles against mighty odds to survive in a harsh landscape. Through her courage, passion, and resourcefulness, the shabbily-dressed orphan becomes a cherished leader of a family and her community, the village of Avonlea. She wins her battle with the rugged Canadian wilderness and earns the right to take her place in the world. This story is seen as a parallel to Canada's experience in the world community.

"Identity" is sometimes too broad a concept to be useful. It does click, however, in a breakdown of the character of Wart in *The Once and Future King*, since his identity as King Arthur goes from buried secret to nation-changing fulfillment. Identity is clearly the main engine of the story, and your instructor will reward you for mentioning it (I would, anyway). You want to go further, and compare Wart to characters in other identity stories that may seem different, while at heart they are the same – Superman, for example, or Celie in *The Color Purple*. In poetry, identity is a widely-seen theme. Maya Angelou's thrilling "Still I Rise," W. E. Henley's classic "Invictus," and Emily Dickinson's introspective "On a Columnar Self" all reflect a search for identity. Another example is James W. Hall's perfect poem, "Maybe Dat's Your Pwoblem Too," a student favorite. Identity is a good key to unlock the puzzle of why this poem is so compelling.

"Assassins' Creed"-style helmeted warrior. Wikimedia Commons.

THE OTHER

Identity often comes in defining who we are not, as well as who we are.

Who we are *not* is the Other.

For there to be an us, there has to be an Other. The Other has no name, no particulars, no childhood, we don't care about his or her clothing or hygiene or motivations or existence in general. The rifle-bearing Native Americans on horseback who threaten the wagon train in Stagecoach are Others; so are the Mexican soldiers who fall in waves in "The Alamo," and the mass of black warriors who overrun the few, brave British soldiers in "Zulu."

In-bred horror-story monsters from the remote hills are Others. Zombies are Others, and may represent an entire class of people – AIDS patients, the mentally ill, society's brainless consumers, etc. In a detective story, the *femme fatale* or seductress is an Other – she exists only to threaten the protagonist (a character with many particulars, who likes black coffee, smokes cigarettes, wears blue ties, cracks ironic jokes, drives too fast, etc.), and then to be overcome by him. Beyond her beauty and capacity for betrayal, the temptress figure has no identity that would make us care about her.

The frequency of the Other's appearance in our literature tends to rise and intensify during wartime – it pays to "Otherize" one's enemies. It is much harder to kill an enemy with whom you empathize.

THE HUMAN CONDITION

This is another favorite phrase of English teachers like me, and it can mean pretty much anything you like. "Green Eggs and Ham" addresses the human condition, but *Of Mice and Men* much more so. John Steinbeck's short, unforgettable story leaves a reader like me aching with heartbreak over our need to love, and our tendency to destroy that which we love.

Revealing this mysterious phrase is the point of all literature, you could argue, and all works reflect some shard of it. Broadly seen, the human condition includes those essentials which all living things share – birth, struggle, love, understanding, success, failure, death. To me, the phrase comes bound up in irony and sadness and unexpected, complex moments of meaning. We all seek happiness, or connection, yet we stumble in our journey to find it, and don't understand why. Maybe children's literature gives us glimpses of the human condition, while adult literature documents our experience of it, I don't know.

CHAPTER THREE
The Building Blocks of Literature

Maxfield Parrish "The Lantern Bearers" (1908)

As you and I seek to break down children's literature, and to understand what makes a story or an author tick, here is a useful index of story components which smart readers and literary critics use to appraise stories.

Plot refers to the story's sequence of physical events, what the characters do, where they go, whom they fight, what actually happens. An Agatha Christie mystery is high on plot, plot twists, surprises, trap-door endings, etc. In my own writing, I find that I always want to ruin a character in order to fulfill the plot – not good. Characters should appear to roam free and act independently. The plot events must come in artfully, unannounced. Once they happen, they should appear inevitable.

Symmetry refers to plots which are the same on both ends – plots in which the punishment for an evil action matches that evil, and the good events balance or mirror the bad events. Events and emotions from the story's beginning are returned to in the end, in proportion. If The Punisher's entire extended family is murdered in the first act, then he must murder the entire family of bad guys in the third act. Humans tend to like symmetry – eyes that are symmetrical on a face, or Frank Lloyd Wright's Robie and Oak Park homes, which have the same mass on both sides. I am a conservative reader, and tend to like old-fashioned, symmetrical structures. Much of contemporary literature is not that way.

Setting refers to the world in which the story take place. An effective author shows the reader the specifics of a time and place, often do with landscape and the natural world, but also the historical context. J.R.R. Tolkien's stories are off the 'setting' charts, with vivid and varied Middle Earth locations.

Character may be the one story element that counts most. The penalty for failing to create believable characters is dire. As film critic William Bibbiani writes about one of the Star Wars films:

> "The Rise of Skywalker" plays like a succession of bullet points: Some of them might be interesting in a vacuum, but **the film never lets its characters demonstrate the emotional depth necessary to carry the audience** from one of those big moments to the next, so every scene that's supposed to blow our minds -- which is practically all of them -- falls completely flat.

Some authors like each character to representing an idea. Main characters usually start out with a need to fill, or a conflict to resolve. Devices or strategies that authors use to build character include physical traits (a scar, a limp), a habit (tucking her hair behind her ears), a sympathetic backstory, hidden fears or quirks, a trademark saying. I often try to stack the odds against my characters, so readers will root for her.

The best characters change over the course of a story.

Theme is a story's underlying meaning. It is why the author wrote it. The main idea, the central concept or message – often unstated. George Lucas has said that the central theme of *Star Wars* is the danger of trusting government.

Sometimes, the storyteller doesn't quite understand his or her own story's theme. Here is the co-author of the phenomenally successful musical, *Fiddler on the Roof*, Jerry Bock, speaking on NPR on the importance of that work's theme:

> *When Jerome Robbins became our director, we had many, many meetings before we went on to rehearsal. And at each meeting, he started with the same question - what is this show about? And he would say there's something that gives this show its power, and we don't know what it is.*
>
> *And finally, at one of those meetings one of us said hey, you know what this show is about? It's about changing of the way of life of a people in these Eastern European communities, these little towns, these shtetls. And Robbins got very excited about that. He said if that's the case, then what you have to write is a member about traditions because we're going to see those traditions change. And that's so important in the show. Every scene or every other scene will be about whether a tradition changes or whether a tradition remains the same.*

Language refers to the quality of the writing, to how the story is told. A linguistic style can range from unadorned to richly embroidered. Shakespeare's writing is the absolute height of rich language.

Here are examples from Ernest Hemingway (famous for deceptively simple, unencumbered prose)

> *He picked up the two heavy bags and carried them around the station to the other tracks.*
>
> *He looked up the tracks but could not see the train.*

and Joseph Conrad (famous for overly long sentences)

And now, dull as they were to the subtle influences of surroundings, they felt themselves very much alone, when suddenly left unassisted to face the wilderness; a wilderness rendered more strange, more incomprehensible by the mysterious glimpses of the vigorous life it contained.

Here is how one of my favorite books, *A Clockwork Orange*, begins. Author Antony Burgess' language here is like none other:

"What's it going to be then, eh?"

There was me, that is Alex, and my three droogs, that is Pete, Georgie, Dim. Dim being really dim, and we just sat in the Korova Milkbar making up our rassodocks what to do with the evening, a flip dark chill winter bastard though dry.

Such different approaches to written language!! All good!!

Dialogue is an important component of any story, written or spoken, and a most useful means by which an author can convey character. Dialogue varies widely, from Shakespeare's long monologues and witty repartee to the terse, ping-pong dialogue of detective stories.

Imagery refers to the representations, or impressions, that illuminate a story. These are usually visual images -- almost symbols, since they carry extra value, or extra meaning -- but they can also be sensory. When I close my eyes and think of *A Thousand Cranes*, I see images of lighted paper lanterns rising in the night sky. John Le Carre ended one of his spy stories with the image of a tire rolling freely down a road, and I still remember it forty years later.

Anagnorisis is an extremely useful term that my students avoid using because it sounds too fancy. It refers to the moment of clarity in a story, a moment of recognition when the hero suddenly understands the real truth – things as they truly stand. The most famous example of anagnorisis: *"Luke, I am your father."*

CHAPTER FOUR
Gender

Wikimedia Commons

Girls and women have been drastically under-represented in Kid Lit, at all levels – even in picture books about animals. Jennie Yabroff, writing in the *Washington Post*, cites a 2011 Florida State University study which found that just 7.5 percent of nearly 6,000 picture books published between 1900 and 2000 depict female animal protagonists. Yabroff goes on to point out the irony behind the scenes:

> **The paradox is that children's literature as we know it was largely created by women.** In the 1930s, educator Lucy Sprague Mitchell formed a writers workshop to produce children's books, launching the careers of writers and illustrators including Margaret Wise Brown

("Goodnight Moon") and Esphyr Slobodkina ("Caps for Sale"). Powerful editors such as Ursula Nordstrom and the influential librarian Anne Carroll Moore shaped the reading habits of children for much of the 20th century. Today, the industry continues to be female-dominated, yet the manuscripts they edit and sell aren't.

Alison Flood, writing in *The Guardian*, notes that "from *The Very Hungry Caterpillar* to *The Cat in the Hat*, *Peter Rabbit* to *Babar*, children's books are dominated by male central characters." This gender disparity in children's literature, whether intended or not, sent children a clear message about which gender carries more value in society.

One brief exception was the spate of 'orphaned girls' stories that became popular early in the 20th Century -- *Heidi* (1880) by Joanna Spyri, *Rebecca of Sunnybrook Farm* (1903) by Kate Douglas Wiggin, and *Pollyanna* (1913) by Eleanor H. Porter, among others.

Equally important as the presence of female characters is their role within the children's story. The hero's mother in *Treasure Island*, the book's lone female, appears only briefly (and sadly) in the opening chapter. Love interest characters can range widely, from active partner to passive object of desire. Female sidekicks often exist to serve and support the male hero in his journey of discovery and overcoming odds. One of the most vivid of these girl-enablers is the "manic pixie dream girl," a term coined by film critic Nathan Rubin to describe the bubbly flight attendant played by Kirsten Dunst in the 2005 film *Elizabethtown*. She is the magical agent who serves a story by ushering the male hero into adulthood (then vanishing). Screenwriter Max Landis has a term, "Mary Sue," for the recurring wish-fulfillment female character who stands in for the audience -- or the writer -- and can do no wrong.

One 'test' or often applied to movie narratives is the Bechdel test. Named after the cartoonist Alison Bechdel, it asks: *Does the story have at least two women who talk to one another about something other than a man?* Many (if not most) movies flunk this test. Try and name three movies which pass this test.

FEMALE CHARACTERS AND DIFFERENCE THEORY

Female characters are more than just male characters with longer hair and different bodies: they need to speak and act in ways that are distinct from males. A researcher named Deborah Tannen has examined genders and finds the two so different that you could almost call males and females two separate cultures: their speech reflects different views of the world, and different underlying values. You don't have to agree with any of this, but you need to begin assessing female and male characters in stories, and how they are portrayed. Here are several 'difference theory' examples.

Status vs. support ... Tannen states that, for men, the world is a competitive place in which conversation and speech are used to build status ("one up" or "one down") whereas, for women, the world is a network of connections. That they use language to seek and offer support.

Orders vs. proposals ... Men will use direct imperatives ("close the door", "switch on the light") when speaking to others. Women encourage the use of super-polite forms, however ("Let's", "Would you mind if ...?").

The gender imbalance in children's literature persists. Of TIME magazine's 2015 list of "100 Best Children's Books of All Time," only 53 books contained female characters who spoke!! A 2016 video entitled "The Ugly Truth of Children's Books, authors Elena Favilli and Francesca Cavallo conducted a library experiment and found that out of over 500 children's books, only one-fourth even contained female characters.

A reader must still ask this question of every children's story: *Do boys and girls read it the same?* Not a few readers have wondered if Hermione Granger, not Harry Potter, is J.K. Rowling's true hero.

NON-TRADITIONAL GENDER PORTRAYALS

Beyond male and female, children's literature has expanded to include portrayals of queer and trans characters in such books as Jill Twiss' A *Day in the Life of Marlon Bundo* and *I am Jazz*, by Jessica Herthel and Jazz Jennings.

Queer theory,' a term coined by Italian-American feminist theorist Teresa de Lauretis, is a prism through which scholars examine literary texts. Queer theorists scorn traditional definitions of "homosexual" and "heterosexual," according to Dinitia Smith in *The New York Times*. They argue that there should be is no strict demarcation between male and female, and that sexuality exists on a continuum.

CHAPTER FIVE
The Three-Act Structure

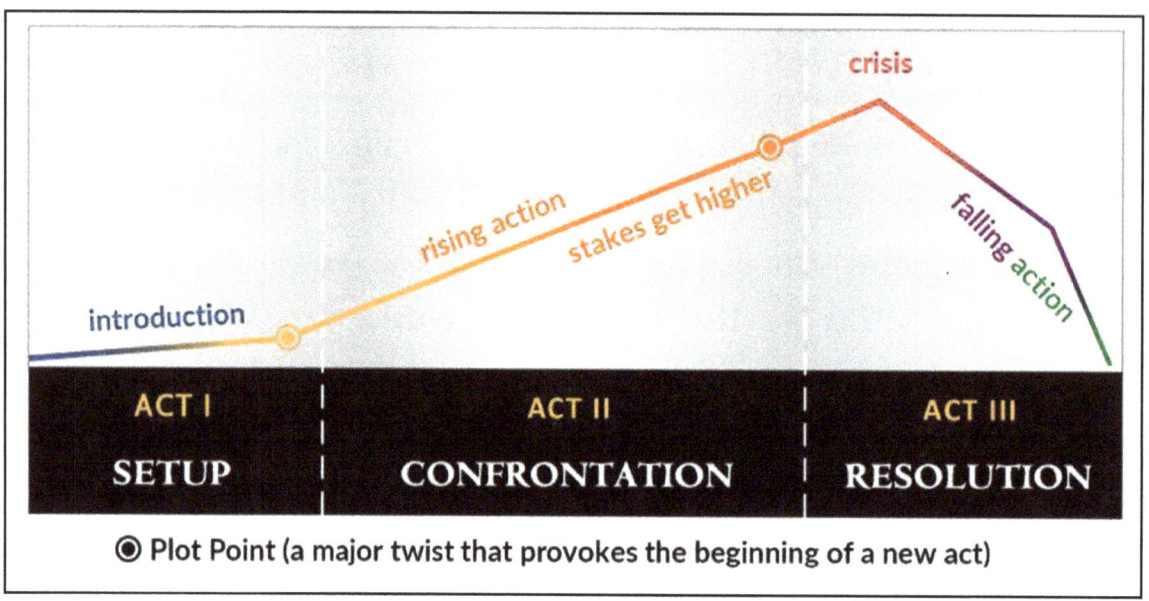

Chart: Gabriel Moura, Elements of Cinema

Most movie screenplays follow a three-act model, which can be applied to books as well. This is the outline or structure that holds the story's characters and events within a movie together, and keeps them in motion: Setup, Rising Action, and Resolution.

Act I: The Setup

Exposition --Introducing the characters, their relationships, and the dynamics of their world. We meet the main character and understand his or her dramatic situation.

Protagonist --the person in the story who has a need/objective to fulfill and whose actions drive the story.

Dramatic premise--what the story's about *(An evil ring will soon destroy or enslave the Shire and everyone else in Middle Earth!)*

Inciting Incident--an event that sets the plot of the film in motion. It occurs approximately halfway through the first act *(The arrival of those rude dwarves)*.

This first turning point ensures that life will never be the same again for the protagonist. It raises a dramatic question that will be answered in the climax of the film *(Can the Fellowship destroy the ring?)*.

A second turning point, or reversal, thrusts the plot in a new direction. Often, the action which leads into Act II is the moment when the hero takes on the problem *(I will visit Mordor and destroy the ring)*.

Act II: Rising Action

Act II is the longest section of the film. It is here that the protagonist and friends learn how incapable they are of solving this terrible dilemma, and learn new skills to do just that. They fail a lot. Their characters develop and change as they effort this impossibly high goal.

Obstacles--In the second act, the main character encounters obstacle (those dark spirits on horseback) after obstacle (raving orc armies) after obstacle (giant spiders) that prevent her or him from achieving his dramatic need.

First Culmination--a point just before the halfway point of the film where the main character seems close to achieving his or hergoal/objective. Then, everything falls apart.

Act III: Crisis and Surprising Resolution

Crisis = A betrayal leads to a new low and the revelation of the real problem, which is actually much worse than anyone thought *(The ring is eating me! And Gandalf is dead!)*

The main character has completely failed (or seems to fail). Heavy doubt arrives.

Climax -- The point at which the plot reaches its maximum tension and the forces in opposition confront each other at a peak of physical or emotional action. *(Gollum and Frodo fight on Mount Doom).*

Denouement: the brief "falling action" period of calm at the end of a film, in which all subplots are resolved and a state of equilibrium returns *(The Shire is safe. Sam is getting married. A pretty ship arrives to take Frodo to his destiny. Gandalf is back).*

See if your next movie does (or does not) follow these Three Act rules.

CHAPTER SIX

Class and Trauma

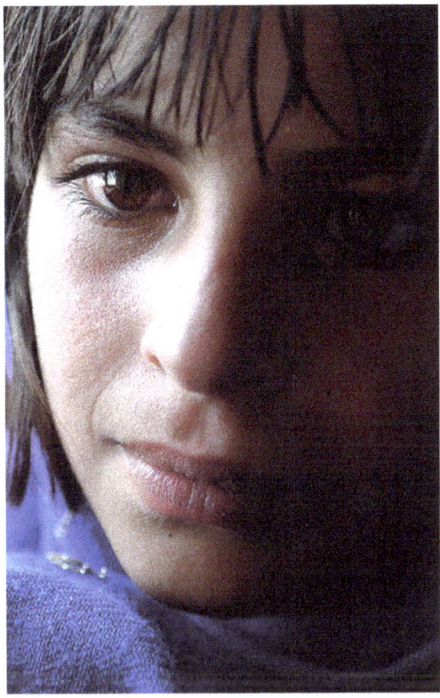

Wikimedia Commons

CLASS CONFLICT IN KID LIT

A popular and persistent theme in children's literature is class conflict. From *A Christmas Carol* (and all of Charles Dickens) to S.E. Hinton's *The Outsiders*, readers can see a mistrust of anyone wealthy as well as tension and misunderstanding between the working class and the landed classes. Protagonists often dream of joining the upper class, where life is easier. Tiny Tim, Pony Boy, Mowgli, Huck Finn, Tom Canty in *The Prince and the Pauper*, as well as Scrooge McDuck and princess characters like Jasmine all encounter the gulf between the social classes. The story of Cinderella looks at first to be a sweet love story, but social critics see an economically-based fantasy about change of status, as a servant girl longs to be chosen by a rich male to join the gentry.

Snow White and *Sleeping Beauty* are prime examples of class-based fairy tales – more specifically, these are tales of yearning to join the ruling class. Both heroines have only one desire – to marry a prince. It is a powerful message, one that has resonated across generations, thanks in part to Disney's extended record of success with princess protagonists.

In works like *Richie Rich*, *Willy Wonka and the Chocolate Factory* and *The Jungle Book*, the existence of a ruling class does not at first seem like a particularly bad thing, but by the time teen readers encounter *The Hunger Games*, the money distance between the oppressed districts and the decadent Capitol are worthy of revolution. The Hunger Games themselves represent a replaying of class struggle ("the dark days of the past"). The role of the books' heroine, Katniss Everdeen, is to revive open class warfare. She temporarily joins the corrupt world of the elite, becoming a painted bird in the gilded cage, before returning to her forest-warrior-self (unlike Bella in *Twilight*, who leaves behind her police chief Dad to take a permanent seat among the vampire nobility).

> **Snow White and Sleeping Beauty are tales not of love, but of a yearning to join the ruling class.**

Philosopher Slavoj Zizeck points out that class conflict can appear even in horror narratives. "Vampires are rich, they live among us," he writes. "Zombies are the poor, living dead, ugly, stupid, attacking from the outside." I would add 2019's *Us* and *The Purge* films as class-conflict horror stories, two films that scare audiences in different ways about the same thing: social inequality.

Class can be a valuable critical tool. Readers may have to look hard, but elements like the upper-class British accent on 90% of villains, and the ubiquitous nasty rich kid in high school stories let us know that class conflict is often present in the structure and subtext of children's stories.

WRITING TRAUMA

One easily recognizable idea that you might find helpful is the idea of "writing trauma."

Scholar Kali Tal in her pioneering book *Worlds of Hurt* and Cornell professor Dominick LaCapra suggest that some of our most powerful stories come from us trying to mend a trauma, or wound, by writing a new version of the trauma story. This applies to individuals – a writer trying to come to terms with a childhood tragedy, for instance – or an event buried in a nation's past (the Vietnam War, 9/11) or an entire segment of collective history (slavery). Revisiting the past to clear away the cobwebs of trauma is a popular theme in kid lit -- we keep retelling the story until we can figure it out, and explain it to ourselves, and make peace with it.

> **Weird goings-on in the present day almost invariably lead to a sin or trauma buried in the past.**

Traumatized youth protagonists like Stephen King's *Carrie* are common in young-adult fiction, with sibling death, high school bullying, car crashes and dysfunctional parents as common causes of the lead character's trauma. You will get a higher grade on your "Watchmen" essay if you mention the idea that the HBO adaptation of the property became a story of trauma, not superheroes, specifically the traumatic legacy of American slavery. Many horror movies gain their meaning from reiterating ghostly or unresolved-from-the-past traumas. Weird goings-on in the present day almost invariably lead to a sin or trauma buried in the past.

Students will certainly find the trauma / revisiting trauma construct helpful in their consideration of poetry. Great poems like Adrienne Rich's "Diving in the Wreck" involve revisiting the past to uncover a trauma that is unrecognized or misunderstood. Langston Hughes, Virginia Woolf, Maya Angelou and Sylvia Plath are among the many poets who deal eloquently in the realm of trauma.

Arthur Rackham's 'Alice' (1907)

GEOGRAPHY IS DESTINY

The endpaper maps in Peter Pan are not just decoration. A clear sense of geography not only sets the characters in space, but gives meaning and direction to the quest for identity. The hero's relationship to the natural world will be become critical, and all COA protagonists have both a positive and a negative experience with nature. Man's uneasy (i.e., mostly lethal) relationship with domestic and wild animals recurs.

From Tolkien on, epic fantasies turn on the geography of the fictional world. The soothing fountains of Rivendell and the grimy gray caverns of Mordor arguably lend as much to the story as any a character. Beyond setting a snowy scenario, the icy climate takes an active part in Phillip Pullman's *His Dark Materials* books. Forests and cities, canyons and mountains peaks, rivers and thunderstorms can all represent dire obstacles and brilliant hope. Nature is a narrative presence in Tarzan's jungle, Mowgli's jungle, Huck Finn's river journey or Laura Wilder's midwestern plains.

All national stories are bound up in geography, and many personal narratives as well. "Geography is destiny" works with some authors (Jack London, John Steinbeck, Carson McCullers) and falls flat with others (Shakespeare, T.S. Eliot).

CHAPTER SEVEN
Billy Wilder's Rules

Wikimedia Commons

HOW MOVIEMAKERS LOOK AT THEIR WORK

This passage is over the head for some readers, but for others it may be a valuable look behind the curtain. This shows how professional storytellers construct a sold narrative – these are the tactics being used on you, so you might as well get a peek at the playbook.

Here are ten rules for writing a good movie, from a series of interviews with a brilliant director you have never heard of named Billy Wilder. The chances are high that whatever movie or television show you watch tomorrow, the people who tell that story have done so with these rules in mind. You want to peek behind the curtain, and use this knowledge to make your own assessments.

"Treat your audience intelligently," says Billy Wilder. "What movies can do, at their best, is let us in -- they *show* us things, they don't *tell* us."

Wilder's most important rule is also the simplest: *Don't be boring*. That is a deceptive rule, since many crammed-with-action films are actually really boring. Here are his ten rules, followed by my own comments and an example or two.

1. **The audience is fickle**. I don't know what this means. How is this a rule?

2. **Grab 'em by the throat and never let 'em go.** Steven Spielberg is a director who totally understands this rule – his films almost always start with characters in the middle of something and then explain as they go (the invasion of Normandy, a thief stealing a relic in cave). Unfortunately, so does the director of *Jump*, which just gave me a headache.

3. **Develop a clean line of action for your leading character.** Unlike, for instance, *Prometheus*.

4. **Know where you're going.** *Swordfish* had no clue where it was going. Script by committee, which applies to a majority of studio films. The two recent *Sherlock Holmes* movies, for example, seemed to change their mind every twenty minutes.

5. **The more subtle and elegant you are in hiding your plot points, the better you are as a writer**. *Saving Private Ryan,* baby. That movie is like clockwork. When the D-Day scene ends with its vast pan downward onto the name on the back of a single GI's pack, then switches to a close-up of a secretary's face, my cadets are spellbound. I am spellbound, and I have seen it twenty times. Or the scene where Vin Diesel eats a red potato and then breaks the brotherhood's rules and pays the price. Oh, my.

> **What movies can do, at their best, is let us in -- they show us things, they don't tell us.**

6. **If you have a problem with the third act, the real problem is in the first act**. Ninety per cent of all movies fall apart in the third act. It is rare, I think, for a

writer to find legitimate conflicts with depth of meaning. *Babe* is a wonderful movie with three very, very solidly crafted acts, I think.

7. **Let the audience solve a mystery**. Let them add up two plus two. They'll love you forever. The *Harry Potter* films do this, over and over. Readers and audiences are most pleased. In *Saving Private Ryan* we wonder who the old man in the opening cemetery scene might be. We assume it is Tom Hanks (but it's not).

8. **In doing voice-overs, be careful not to describe what the audience already sees. Add to what they're seeing**. I thought at first that this was a minor rule until I began to notice just how many movies have voice-overs.

Blade Runner, a surprisingly good movie (surprising because the first time I saw it I did not like it. I blame myself.) has what Wilder is talking about, this oblique narrative. Another smart and durable movie, *How to Train Your Dragon*, seems to break this rule, but I like it anyway.

9. **The event that occurs at the second act curtain triggers the end of the movie**. In *Saving Private Ryan*, when the regiment of rescuers encounters the German tank and obliterates it, the unexpected result is that, at the only moment they are not trying to find Private Ryan, they find him. Surprise! Cut straight to the final act – the fateful bridge at Ramelle. Super sturdy storytelling.

> **If Act III is weak, the real problem is Act 1 …**

10. **The third act must build, build, build in tempo and action until the last event, and then -- that's it. Don't hang around**. Franco Zeffirelli's abridged film version of *Hamlet* (which features one of the handsomest sets ever) does this well, wisely resisting the temptation to make long speeches when the action is over. The third *Lord of the Rings* film hung around so long I wanted to grade papers, anything.

You can see Billy Wilder's rules in action in his own films, which include *Double Indemnity*, *Some Like It Hot* and *Sunset Boulevard*.

CHAPTER EIGHT

Images of War in Children's Literature

The London WWII bombings, an image recurring in such Kid Lit as 'Harry Potter'

Many children's stories are also war stories.

Some portray explicit wars, such as young adult novels *The Book Thief*, *Johnny Tremain*, *The Summer of My German Soldier*, *Code Name Verity*, *Sadako and The Thousand Paper Cranes*, and Gary D. Schmidt's *Okay for Now* among a legion of others. Many other youth-driven narratives use a masked version of war as not only a backdrop or framing device, but also for its particular images and dramatic structures. *Star Wars*, the *Harry Potter* books and all of the Avengers movies, for instance.

Book series like *Divergent* and *The Maze Runner* (and many dystopic stories) are structured on a futuristic rebellion in the model of the American Revolution, with brave outgunned young patriots rising up against a giant, ruthlessly evil empire. James Cameron's *Avatar*, one of the most-watched movies ever, is an explicit recapitulation of the American colonial wars, this time with the natives winning.

The later titles of the *Harry Potter* series veer into explicit World War II war scenarios, complete with Dumbledore's Army, with its echoes of the French Resistance, a deeply embedded secret agent (Snape), and a secret society reminiscent of Kim Philby. The climactic Siege of Hogwarts surely draws from the WWII siege of London, with images of toppling brick walls and smudged survivors walking, dazed, among the rubble. These are images straight from 1944 newsreels.

The Avengers series is tied to 9/11 – repeated surprise aerial attacks by 'aliens,' the imagery of falling buildings in city downtowns, heroes squinting in the smoke and debris. Perhaps more than any other war model, it is Hiroshima which lurks beneath the surface of all the superhero movies, the dominant Kid Lit of our time. Surely the red cube or World Destroying Thing is a stand-in for the nuclear bomb, in the early 1940's, when both Germany and the Allies were racing after it. Elsewhere in the Marvel universe, Captain America is all things World War II, while Nick Fury can be seen as a representative of the Cold War era. Representing more contemporary wars, the villain Ultron seems like a personification of cyber war.

Wikimedia Commons

The *Twilight* books feature a Roman command structure, including an aristocratic tribunal and a battlefield conference between opposing sides, in which a dream-battle shows the imperial Volturi that they must give it up.

The Lord of the Rings should be World War I, but it isn't, not really. J.R.R. Tolkien was a Medieval scholar, and he may have patterned his thousand-page war fantasy of cavalries, archers, and clashing monarchies after stories like *The Song of Roland* and Teutonic myths. I don't see traces of trench warfare or poison gas from the Battle of the Somme in the Hobbit epics. Tolkien's grandson, Christopher, disagrees, writing that the parallels between the hobbit epic and World War I are obvious:

> Evil in Middle Earth is above all industrialised. Sauron's orcs are brutalised workers; Saruman has 'a mind of metal and wheels'; and the desolate moonscapes of Mordor and Isengard are eerily reminiscent of the no man's land of 1916.

Star Wars famously modeled its space dogfights on those of the Battle of Britain in World War II. We can also see in the Ewok skirmishes echoes of natives protecting their forests against industrialized invaders (like Hobbits, the Ewoks are re-enacting the opposition from the war for the American West). While details of the overall Rebel-Alliance-versus-Galactic-Empire war remain vague, we can speculate that the Death Star is a reflection of what the Bismarck was supposed be in World War II, and that the command-center scenes echo those of WWII films like *Battle of the Bulge* and *The Longest Day*. The Darth Vader character seems like a combination of a Hitler figure and a symbol of nuclear war (J. Robert Oppenheimer, one of the fathers of Project Manhattan, quoted the Bhagavad Gita, "Now I am become Death, Destroyer of Worlds …").

As *Peter Pan* builds to climactic, good-form battle with Hook versus the young and the colonized, so does *The Wind in the Willows* culminate in a battle (this one against that thieving band of local weasels). These high-empire battles represent a quaint idea of combat, an old-fashioned, pre-Omdurman bloodless interchange that is more like a party gone wild than the tank battle at Kursk.

I'm not sure if Mowgli's extended duel with Shere Khan in Rudyard Kipling's *The Jungle Book* is war, but it is certainly combat, involving both strategy and tactics. Once again, higher (or better) intelligence wins out.

CHAPTER NINE
Empire

Ernest Shephard, from "The Wind in the Willows"

This is the least crucial of all the sections of this book.

Looking at the presence of empire in literature is of great interest to me and my students, but a consideration of empire is not a must-have critical tool for you. The idea is simple: historians like Niall Ferguson see history as a rising and falling of empires. Cultures and economies wage war, as well as armies and navies. Literary scholar Edward Said set out a theory of Orientalism, which sees literature as a battlefield where these clashing cultures vie for dominance. The 'winning' culture then steals the stories of the 'conquered.' When Spanish missionaries invaded the Yucatan, the first thing they did was to burn the Maya's 'pagan' writings (Bishop Diego de Landa in 1562). This helped assure that Christian writings would win out. Who tells the stories matters.

In obvious ways and in subtle ways, children's literature reflects the cultural battles of empire. Laura Ingalls Wilder's *Little House on the Prairie* books are a do-it-yourself account of how America's western empire rose, farm by farm, and the Shoshone who threaten Pa's wheat field do not get a fair share of the story. The story is how immigrants built America, and Native Americans are mostly extras in that epic.

See what you think of the following chart and breakdown. If it gives you a headache, skip it and go to Part Two, in which some very smart scholars give you in-depth analysis of *Tarzan*, *Binti*, *The Lion King*, *Star Wars* and more.

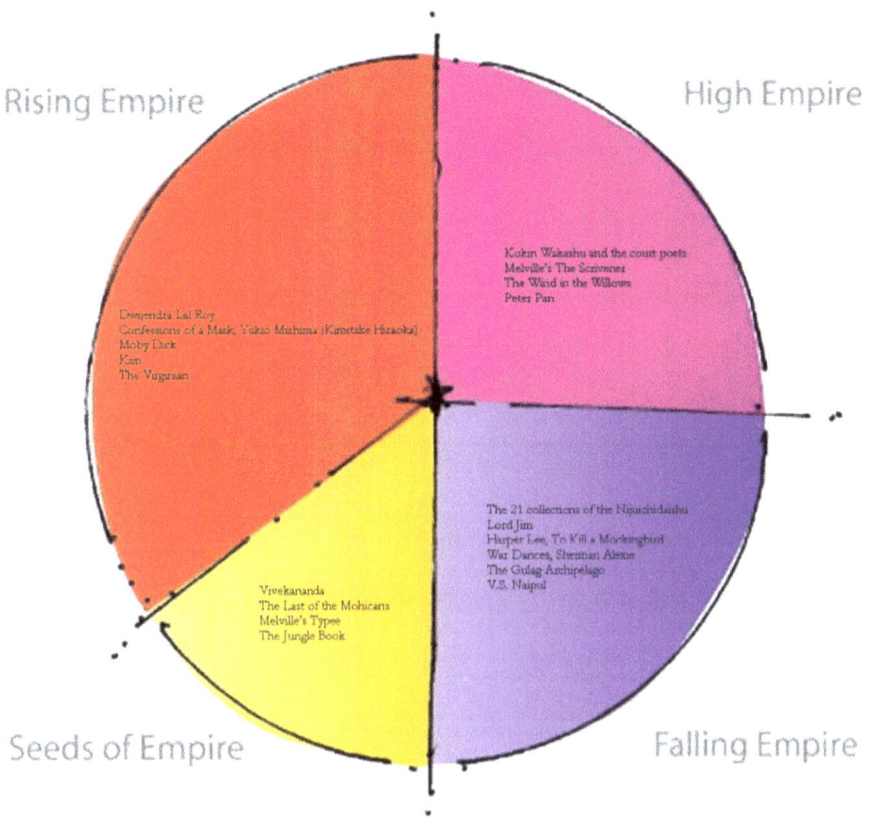

There exist very few legitimate **Stage One: Roots of Empire** children's stories. *Robinson Crusoe* is certainly one of those, where the two cultures meet on equal terms. The narrative quickly moves into **Stage Two: Rising Empire**, where the white man wields superior technology (a pistol) and takes command of the black man. Scott O'Dell's *Island of the Blue Dolphins*, William Golding's remarkable *Lord of the Flies*, and *The Travels of Jaimie McPheeters* by Robert Lewis Taylor might be others.

There are many more **Stage Two: Rising Empire stories** – in which one race begins to hold sway over 'subservient' cultures. Both Tarzan and Mowgli begin early in their stories to assert a natural 'superiority' over even the biggest, strongest animals in the jungle world. There is a clear caste system in these allegorical tales. George Orwell's wonderful *Animal Farm* is a case study in Stage Two.

A book like Kenneth Grahame's *The Wind in the Willows* is a glowing example of **High Empire** (Quadrant Three) children's literature, a celebration of all the joys of empire (tea from India, sophisticated banter, imported food, poetry, mechanized toys, laundresses, doing battle against foes of inferior breeding) with no reference to its underlying complexities. Huck Finn, during his adventures alongside the slave Jim, certainly questions the premise of slavery, which is a flagstone of high empire.

The highest deed of high empire is defending the nation against a rival force, so *The Red Badge of Courage* and all war stories are High Empire. The *Harry Potter* canon is filled with shards of empire. Not merely that the fall of the British Empire can be seen in the fall of Hogworts, but, on a much larger scale, the oppositions – the dueling hierarchies of good and evil (the British and German officer corps), for example -- the characters, and the class structures derive from historical empires. We can't help it.

Along with the children's stories of Rudyard Kipling, European kids' properties like *Babar*, *Asterix*, *Curious George* and *Tintin* are mentioned as imperial tales which reinforce the colonial structure. Tintin is part of the European narrative, the story that European cultures tell about themselves and their place in the world. Class, race and slavery are part of that story.

There is currently a glut of young-adult **Stage Four: Falling Empire** children's literature. *The Hunger Games* and all dystopian y.a. narratives fit this category.

The central message of a Stage Four story is this: we blew it. Internal corruption sunk the imperial systems, and now we are left with the bitter, polluted, oligarchical dregs of an after-world, where honest kids don't stand a chance. *The Little Prince* is probably at the very beginning of Stage Four. He is powerfully lamenting some lost quality: the empire is no longer noble, it is starting to crumble from within. I cannot decide if S.E. Hinton's smart, durable, teenaged-misfits fiction is the last gasp of High Empire or the beginnings of Falling Empire.

A brilliant scholar named Nalini Iyer writes about 'masked fiction,' domestic dramas like The Secret Garden or *The Little Princess* in which the dynamics of empire are evident. As manpower ran the empire, women ran the household, and many of these home-based stories play out imperial themes, from intrigue among the Indian serving staff to a struggle over who controls land (the walled garden).

This process of war among the narratives is not a conspiracy, or intentionally evil, it happens whenever cultures clash. Then the cycle turns, and new stories and new writers come along to correct the false images, to fill in the gaps where entire populations have been overlooked. Tales of the Christian empire replaced those of the Roman Empire, as one empire displaced another. In the end, empire is secondary in our consideration of Kid Lit. The prime directive of children's literature is to explain the family, and then the world.

> **Every empire regularly tells itself and the world that it is unlike all other empires, and that it has a mission, certainly not to plunder and control, but to educate and liberate the peoples and places it rules directly or indirectly.**
>
> *-- Edward Said*

PART TWO
In Depth Studies
TEN STUDIES

Maxfield Parrish, 'Arabian Nights' (1909)

Note from Tom

The second section of this book, "In Depth," is more challenging than the first section. Scholars write for other scholars, so in this prose and in these interviews, the ideas and references come fast and furious.

I urge readers to give it a try. Teachers can assign just the introduction, or the first question of an interview. I have left markers of the best quotes in headlines, so you can quickly catch each feature article's general drift (identify the thesis, that is).

While the learned references can sometimes serve as a barrier to smooth reading, the reward is worth the effort. These are wonderful ideas which these dedicated young scholars worked hard to reveal. I have tried to select features which both address well-known literary properties and explain that topic in fairly clear prose.

This past summer, I sent out a Call for Papers on Kid Lit and received a wealth of replies, so these essays and interviews are never-before-seen. At the end of each study is a link to the full feature as it appears in the free, open-access online magazine which I edit, Empire Studies Magazine (www.empirestudies.com)

I do not know enough to write intelligently about two aspects of children's literature – picture books and international lit. Later editions of this book will include more.

Your pal,

Tom D.

CHAPTER TEN

The Lion King and Its Message of Social Darwinism

A Cultural Critic Sees Undertones of Fascism in the Popular Story
Dan Hassler-Forest

Wikimedia Commons

Introduction

In this smart, provocative article and interview, cultural critic Dan Hassler-Forest warns us that loaded images and ideas may lurk beneath the surface of the most innocent-looking story. His thesis is that the widely popular Disney story, *The Lion King* has at its heart a love (or at least an acceptance) of fascism. The inherited right of Simba and Mufasa to lord it over the lower animals of the veldt is presented as a fact, and their absolute authority is never questioned.

Dan Hassler-Forest is far from alone in his consideration of tyranny as it appears in children's literature. A surprising number of dissertations delve into the wizarding world of Harry Potter and its portrayal of tyrannical villainy (Valdemort is characterized by scholars as the equivalent of a wizard Hitler) as well as the chokehold which the oppressive Ministry of Magic puts on Hogworts. Author J.K. Rowling includes explicit thinking on the subject in *Harry Potter and the Half-Blood Prince*:

> *Voldemort himself created his worst enemy, just as tyrants everywhere do! Have you any idea how much tyrants fear the people they oppress? All of them realize that, one day, amongst their many victims, there is sure to be one who rises against them and strikes back!*

Other young-reader narratives engage the question of tyrants and tyranny, often in their depictions of all-powerful villains (*Shadowfell*, *Catching Fire*) and regimes (*A Handmaid's Tale*, *1984*, *Fahrenheit 451*). In his riveting, tragic novel about schoolboys abandoned on an island, *Lord of the Flies*, William Golding gives young readers a chillingly clear message. He shows how the well-meaning boys begin in democracy and, good faith and then, step by agonizing step, descend into tyranny. George Orwell's remarkable "Animal Farm" offers a similarly bleak portrait of communism.

An arguably more pro-tyrant children's story is Roald Dahl's 1964 novel, *Charlie and the Chocolate Factory* (adapted to screen in 1971 as *Willy Wonka and the Chocolate Factory*). In this fascinating fantasy, an all-powerful, bizarre dictator and candy baron dictates matters of life, death, and destiny, without anyone questioning his authority.

> **There is a very obvious caste system in *The Lion King*, which is not only clearly visible, but which is also enormously rigid.**

Hamlet Comparison *The Lion King* is a favorite for interpretation by scholars like me. One line of thought compares Simba's story to that of Shakespeare's tragic hero, Hamlet. Like Hamlet's father, Mufasa is murdered by his own brother, who wants to take the throne. Like the Prince of Denmark, the Prince of the Savannah first runs from his responsibilities ("Hakuna matata") after his father's death, but later returns to avenge that death. In the end of both tales, the evil uncles wind up dead, though Simba shows more mercy than Hamlet.

The Lion King **as a Christian text**. Other scholars see biblical echoes in *The Lion King* Jonathan Barfield of "Philosophy Now" points out that the relationship between Mufasa and Simba mirrors that between God the Father and Jesus the Son. Rafiki the baboon says, "He lives in you." Similarly, God lives in us, and is always watching over us.

When Simba says, "I just needed to get out on my own, live my own life, and I did, and it's great," Bible scholars see strong similarities to Jesus's Parable of the Prodigal Son (Luke 15:11 32). In the parable, the son thinks he can live better without the responsibilities he has while living with his family, and so leaves to live in a 'far country'. This is exactly how Simba behaves, before returning as a savior figure.

62 | *Kid Lit: An Introduction to Literary Criticism*

Rembrandt's portrayal of the Bible parable, "The Prodigal Son," which bears some similarity to The Lion King plot.

Interview with Dan Hassler-Forest
August, 2019

1. What are three ideas you would like young viewers of *The Lion King* to consider?

If we're talking about young children: they are still working to make sense of the world, and the roles that may be available to them in it. Many Disney movies offer them narrative frameworks that help them imagine what it means to move from childhood to adulthood. A question to ask them to consider would be: what does it mean to grow up? What kinds of adult behavior does the story provide? For teens and young adults, there is a stronger awareness of how society is organized, and how their behavior is constrained by power relationships. For them, it is more useful to ask how power is organized in this society, how it relates to their own experience of the world, and whether the worldview on display in the film is (or isn't) compatible with their own values. This could help them draw their own conclusions about how social and political structures are reproduced through popular media and children's stories.

> **Disney movies offer children narrative frameworks that help them imagine what it means to move from childhood to adulthood.**

2. How would you re-write TLK to ameliorate the 'fascist' problem at its core? If Pixar had made it, how would TLK be different?

One thing that could at least make the problem more visible would be to tell the story from the hyenas' point of view. If we were to follow a young hyena cub whose hopes and dreams of leading a decent life had been eroded by being forcefully consigned to the margins of society all their life, we would have an entirely different perspective on the lions' autocratic power, and what it means to grow up under the iron boot of tyranny. It's no coincidence that there are no hyena cubs anywhere in the film, as these social outcasts must be seen as deserving of their fate, and never as in any way "innocent." Of course this wouldn't make the organization of the movie's society any less fascist, but it would give us an entirely different perspective on its power structure.

> **Mufasa's pleasant-sounding but profoundly weird "Circle of Life"... provides a very thinly-masked rationale for social Darwinism.**

3. One consideration often noted is that *The Lion King* is basically *Hamlet* – an uneasy prince at the center of murder and intrigue, with Timba and Poomba as Rosencrantz and Guildenstern, Scar as Claudius, and Nala is Ophelia (also, the father returns as a ghost.)

Another interpretation is that TLK is a Christian story (Simba is the Prodigal Son, Scar is Satan, Mufasa is God the Father, and Simba's return to the Pridelands is Jesus's Second Coming), while a third perspective sees the story as an existentialist parable.

Which is 'true'? Are animated movies political? Is it unfair to burden them with too much symbolic meaning? Does it take away from our enjoyment of them?

One of the nicest things about stories is that they are there for us to interpret rather than providing a single fixed meaning. And our interpretation of a story derives from an enormous variety of factors, not least of which the social and cultural context in which we produce them. This explains why many people see many different things in a movie like *The Lion King*. But in my experience, the majority of our interpretations of these kinds of stories tend to be at the level of the individual character (what does Simba learn from his experiences? what parallels can we find in literary and cultural history?) rather than at the political level (what kind of power relationships define the world these characters inhabit? how do they correspond to political systems we know from human history?). So while these more personal interpretations are certainly valid, I try to stimulate students and readers to look at these texts from a more political perspective, in part because it helps them understand how social systems of power reproduce themselves through media.

Hamlet and The Lion King share many plot points.

4. One of the most powerful sentences in your article is this one:

When we consider that Mufasa is really explaining to his own heir why it's perfectly fine to behave dictatorially, the lions' perspective feels a lot more unsettling.

What does that mean? How can young TLK viewers process this idea?

Children have a very strong sense of social justice, so it's very natural for Simba to point out to his father that rather than "respecting" the leaping antelope (as he just explained), they actually eat the antelope. Mufasa's pleasant-sounding but profoundly weird "Circle of Life" answer provides a very thinly-masked rationale for social Darwinism. If we translate it to human terms, it's as if a child asking a rich parent why it's all right for them to be billionaires while other people live in poverty. The father's answer would be something about "maintaining balance" in the world, since a small minority of the rich (the top of the food chain) were simply meant to rule over the poor. Of course, Simba's response is then simply to internalize this ideology, and look forward in great excitement to all the privilege that awaits him once he's all grown up. I think that young viewers would see this tension very easily once they become aware of the fact that the movie isn't really about lions, but about what it means to have enormous power and privilege in the human world. Then asking them what they might do differently from how the Pridelands are organized could lead to interesting conversations about power, ambition, and social justice.

> **There is a very obvious caste system in *The Lion King*, which is not only clearly visible, but which is also enormously rigid.**

5. Is *The Lion King* an African story? An American story? A British story? How would it be different if it had been Chinese?

I would describe it very much as an American story that uses elements from other cultures (especially from African cultures) as a kind of window dressing to make it seem more exotic. In the same way that the Elton John songs featured on the soundtrack are very clearly American pop songs with African-sounding choruses and an occasional line of Swahili thrown in, the story is very much a familiar Western narrative about individualism, family, and personal responsibility with a few dabs of eye-catching but functionally insignificant cultural appropriation. A big difference with many other cultures (including many indigenous mythologies from non-Western contexts) is that there tends to be a much stronger sense of *collective rather than individual identity*. Thus, the strictly hierarchical worldview of *The Lion King*, with the lions at the top and the hyenas at the bottom, would most likely be much less present in a Chinese telling of a similar tale. (See also this article by Ida Yoshinaga on cultural appropriation in Disney's *Moana*.)

6. Is there a class or caste system among the animals in *The Lion King*? How does this compare to societies in other Disney movies, such as *Bambi* and *The Jungle Book*?

Yes, there is a very obvious caste system in *The Lion King*, which is not only clearly visible, but which is also enormously rigid. The problem, again, is that clearly identifiable human social groups are depicted metaphorically as animal species organized as a "food chain": predators (lions), prey (herbivores), and poachers (hyenas). Whereas actual hyenas are predators and lions are matriarchal in their social structures, these fictionalized depictions of animals make *The Lion King* into an allegory for a form of class struggle in which the hyenas are the only ones who are unsatisfied with the organization of power. *Bambi* has a similar focus on patriarchal traditions, in which men have all the authority and women only exist as maternal nurturers. But it doesn't use animal species as metaphors for class distinctions – in part because the story's world also includes humans, and the deer, rabbits, and other cute and cuddly characters are more literally animals. The same thing holds true for *The Jungle Book*, which is seen by many as racist for using King Louie and his monkeys as ethnically coded minority characters who dream of being white and powerful ("I Wanna Be Like You"), but in which predators like Shere Khan are certainly not pictured as divinely appointed authority figures. A more recent film that features a rather complicated use of animal species as allegorical fable figures for human societies is *Zootopia*, where predator-prey relationships are used to foreground issues like racism and sexism.

7. In current children's literature or, more broadly, children's culture (films, games, television), which narratives give you hope for the genre? Which stories worry you?
Hayao Miyazaki's films have always given me hope for the genre: not only have they consistently focused on urgent societal issues like climate change and care for the environment (again, something that children respond very strongly to), but they are always critical and mocking in their depiction of the powerful, and

they focus on compassion and learning rather than competition and romance. Many recent American children's animation series have also offered socially engaged and progressive quality storytelling (*Hilda*, *My Little Pony: Friendship is Magic*, the recent *She-Ra* reboot), all of which playfully and subtly introduce young children to larger social justice issues while also offering appropriate (or at least: inoffensive) role models and stories. I also think the ways in which the Star Wars movies have developed in the past decade provides a very hopeful political direction for this kind of franchise.

8. A huge percentage of parents in children's literature do not make it past the opening scenes. Is all this matricide and patricide too dark for a children's tale?

Fear of abandonment and even more specifically fear of losing a parent is one of the most overwhelming and universal anxieties for children. It's probably not surprising therefore that so many children's stories involve the (temporary) loss of a parent in some way – in part because they help young children imagine what it might be like to be in an intimidating situation without a reliable adult to help them through it. But while there are many ways in which a story can isolate a child and have them fend for themselves, Disney movies have really made the "dead parent trope" into a veritable cliché. I do think that both the oft-repeated pattern of one or more dead parents has been overplayed by Disney features, as has the insistent focus on romantic heterosexual relationships, which young children really have very little interest in.

DAN HASSLER-FOREST'S ESSAY

'The Lion King' is a fascistic story. No remake can change that.

No matter how you look at it, this is a film that introduces us to a society where the weak have learned to worship at the feet of the strong

Link: https://www.washingtonpost.com/outlook/2019/07/10/lion-king-is-fascistic-story-no-remake-can-change-that/

CHAPTER ELEVEN

Star Wars and Government

**The Heart of the Space-Based Franchise Lies in Civics
Alexander Maxwell**

"Cicero in the Roman Senate," a painting by Granger. The Roman Empire is a recurring civic model in modern science fiction.

Editor's Introduction

Without some form of government, we are stuck in Thomas Hobbes' hellish state of nature, 'the war of all against all.' No one wants that. Humans live in tribes, and tribes need a structure, a way to make decisions. Your family has a governing style – your parents can tell you what to do (dictatorship) or ask your opinion (benevolent monarchy) or the family takes a vote (participatory democracy); your sports teams and classrooms have governing models, too.

But which form of government, or civic decision-making, is the right one? Socialism? Communism? Oligarchy? Libertarian democracy? Theocracy? Children's literature has the answer – many answers, actually. From the happy king- and queen-dom of *Cinderella* to the failed island collective of *Lord of the*

Flies to the self-rule of the *Little House on the Prairie* books, we see a wide range of alternatives. "Children's literature makes and educates future citizens," write Christopher Kelen and Bjorn Sundmark in their excellent anthology of essays, "The Nation in Children's Literature." They continue, "the emergence of modern nation-states towards the end of the eighteenth century and the rise of children's literature in the same period is not coincidental." Yow!! Such scholars identify – and rightly so, I think – children's literature as a key component of culture connecting child and nation. Stories about young protagonists portray communities, and those communities all have a specific character.

In the following essay and interview, Alexander Maxwell looks at one of the most influential of young-reader / young-viewer epics and comes away with clever observations about governments in space. His premise is that, beneath the light-sabre fights and spaceships, memorable characters and thrilling adventure, the *Star Wars* movies are all about government: specifically, clashing forms of government, and what they bring to their citizens.

You don't need to believe him. In a 2005 *Chicago Tribune* interview, here is what George Lucas said:

> *[The original* Star Wars*] was really about the Vietnam War, and that was the period where Nixon was trying to run for a [second] term, which got me to thinking historically about how do democracies get turned into dictatorships?*

Nor is Alexander Maxwell the only scholar with opinions on this topic. In his insightful essay, "Why the Politics of the *Star Wars* Universe Makes No Sense," Scott Detrow writes:

> *The Jedi knights may have been a destabilizing force who contributed to the downfall of the Old Republic. They play a very weird and undemocratic role and they're secretive and they're religious and they don't seem to be subject to anybody else's rules other than their own."*

Discussion raged over the Vietnam War. MLK and LBJ. Photo: National Archives

In his paper, "The Road to Hell: *Star Wars* as Criticism of Paternalism as Empire," William Nolen puts forth the idea that in *Star Wars Episode II: the Attack of the Clones* (2002), Anakin and Padme lay out the beginnings of a theocracy – a combination of state and religious power. Eventually, of course. Anakin turns to tyranny, his childhood traumas "presumably pushing him to value order over liberty."

We can also widen the lens and include other literary properties aimed at young readers. *Twilight*, for example, includes a sort of throwback to a Roman Empire model, for example (although the good guys are organized like a United Nation of vampires). The evil government that creeps into the middle and later *Harry Potter* books represents Parliamentary bureaucracy gone out of control, with Sirius Black and the Weasleys opposing it, using an informal military command structure.

As students, you need to begin to notice these governing structures which underlie your favorite stories, films, songs and fantasy games. You have consumed hundreds of hours of these narratives, and you will profit by discerning this aspect among them. As teachers, we need to use the rich subtexts of these popular to initiate students into the world of critical thinking.

Link: http://empirestudies.com/2019/12/16/star-wars-and-government/

Interview with Scholar Alexander Maxwell

October 2019

1. In his article, "Why the Politics of *Star Wars* Make No Sense," Brett Neely concludes that, in terms of government, "The Galactic Senate portrayed in Episodes I-III is a mess." There don't seem to be political parties, he points out, or a second chamber, and one key planet, Naboo, apparently elects its queen, Padmé Amidala (royalty is never elected, in the real world).

I'm not familiar with Neely's article. I wouldn't want to argue that the politics of *Star Wars* make perfect sense, and indeed I noted some problems in my article. However, the particular objections raised in this question don't seem such big problems to me. The lack of a second chamber means nothing: historically, there have been several unicameral parliaments. Insofar as the Galactic Republic contains many planets that enjoy wide-reaching local autonomy, furthermore, we might compare the Galactic Senate to the General Assembly of the United Nations. Delegates to the UN General Assembly represent their respective countries, not political parties. Is it really so strange that the Galactic Republic would resemble the UN General Assembly? I agree that the elected queen of the Naboo is a bit silly; Lucas probably just wanted his female lead to have a fairy-tale style title. Nevertheless, even elected monarchs are not wholly unknown. The Holy Roman Emperor and the Prince of Novgorod were both elected, even if only by elite electors. Parliaments in many different countries have also filled vacant royal thrones through elections.

2. What governmental role do the Jedi knights play? You refer to them as a police force, yet they seem to have wide-ranging, independent role, a sort of secret, semi-religious, enforcer society. Does their role change over the course of the films?

I suspect the Jedi knights are interesting because in the *Star Wars* universe mastering the power of the Force grants supernatural abilities. Jedi knights move objects with their mind, see into the future, communicate telepathically (at the end of Episode V) and even commune with the dead. In the real world, there is no caste of warriors with supernatural abilities, so we cannot expect to find a perfect real-life equivalent to the Jedi Knights.

Knowledge of the Force does indeed have a religious dimension. In Episode IV an imperial officer even describes it as "that ancient religion." The Jedi also resemble a religious order in that Jedi are supposed to be celibate, like monks. They do not, however, seem like a secret society: they wear distinctive clothing, and can easily be recognized on sight. We also learn in Episode I that they can be sent as ambassadors, which seems a pretty public role to me.

In terms of their governmental role, however, their most important quality is that they have placed themselves at the disposal of the Galactic Republic. They are not trying to rule on their own account, they respect the Senate's authority and take orders from the Supreme Chancellor. So, I think it's basically right to think of them as a police force. The Jedi are not numerous to be called an army, even if they make effective officers for clone soldiers. They are respected and influential players in Galactic politics, at least in the first three episodes, but military leaders are often important in political life.

Their role obviously changes when the Galactic Republic collapses and the Jedi go into hiding. It's sort of interesting that the surviving Jedi do not join the Rebellion against the Empire. Had Yoda or Obi-Wan Kenobi wanted to join the Rebel Alliance, one imagines that they would have become respected and influential leaders. Indeed, their withdrawal from politics only makes sense as a plot device.

Disney … seems more interested in the "hero's journey" aspect of the *Star Wars* franchise.

3. The climactic dogfight is often compared to WWII dogfights – do other historical scenarios figure in?

The climactic battle scene at the end of Episode IV closely resembles the climactic battle at the end of the 1955 film Dambusters. If you search YouTube with the keywords "Dambusters Star Wars," you can find a shot-by-shot comparison. Lucas even borrowed some of his dialogue from Dambusters. So, that sequence is not so much based on a historical scenario, but on a movie.

Wikimedia Commons

It's sometimes hard to tell whether something in a film is based on historical events, or on a cinematic depiction of historical events. Given the importance of the Nazis as Hollywood villains, the Nazi imagery in *Star Wars* could perhaps be interpreted not as referencing the German dictatorship, but as referencing Hollywood World War Two films. Either way, however, the moral meaning of the symbolism is clear. It means: "these are the bad guys."

4. Your article looks at the first six films. Do the politics, or the governments, of the current, non-Lucas *Star Wars* change?

It seems to me that Disney doesn't have a very clear vision of the political context in which their stories unfold. They seem more interested in the "hero's journey" aspect of the *Star Wars* franchise. The "First Order" is modeled on Nazi Germany even more strongly than the Galactic Empire, and is thus clearly marked as the bad guys. That said, we don't get a lot of information about how the First Order works, or who supports it, or why. There's some interesting tension between Kylo Ren, the Sith apprentice to Supreme Leader Snoke, and the New Order's military caste. Since Finn is not a clone, furthermore, the First Order apparently recruits its soldiers differently than the Empire did. But that's about all we know. There's even less information about the Resistance. So we know that there's a new political context, but the films don't give us much to analyze.

5. In a 2005 Chicago Tribune interview, George Lucas said that he drew inspiration from the Vietnam War, "the period where Nixon was trying to run for a [second] term, which got me to thinking historically … how do democracies get turned into dictatorships?" Do you see echoes of Vietnam in *Star Wars*?

I personally don't see echoes the Vietnam War. Perhaps it's because I am too young to remember the Vietnam War, or perhaps because I have, as a historian, taken more interest in other places and times. I'm an expert in Central Europe: the "democracy to dictatorship" narrative makes me think of Weimar Germany. A scholar of the classics might instead think about the fall of the Roman Republic. If I were an expert in the Vietnam War era, perhaps I would see the films differently.

That said, I'm surprised to learn Lucas had the Vietnam War era in mind, not least because I don't see the Vietnam War as a moment of transition from democracy to dictatorship. When I first saw the film, I actually assumed Lucas was commenting about then-president George W. Bush and the war in Iraq, specifically because I took the line "so this is how liberty dies – with thunderous applause" as a reference to the 2001 Patriot Act.

6. Can you cite two or three other literary worlds where the political order is an important element of the narrative?

Governments feature prominently in several imaginary worlds. Decisions taken by political leaders can dramatically affect people's lives. It's unsurprising that political leaders appear in fictional worlds.

In the cartoon *Rick and Morty*, for instance, the main characters interact not only with the U.S. president (season 1, episode 5; season 3 episode 10), but also with alien politicians such as Prince Nebulon of the Zigerions (season 1, episode 4), Ma-Sha, the ruler of Gazorpazorp (season 1, episode 7), the unnamed "presidentress of the Megagargantuans" (season 3, episode 10), and so forth. I think *Rick and Morty* expresses a very radical libertarianism, even if the show doesn't articulate its views all that forcefully.

In the *Harry Potter* saga, to give another example, the Ministry of Magic plays an important role. Over the course of the books, we meet several government officials, including two Ministers of Magic. The final novel, *Harry Potter and the Deathly Hallows*, depicts a coup d'etat and its effects on the criminal justice system. J. K. Rowling, who once worked as a researcher for Amnesty International, has a deep understanding of political violence. The Harry Potter series has a pretty sophisticated take on the moral questions such violence raises.

> "Rick and Morty" expresses a very radical libertarianism ...

7. Why should young viewers care about all this? What does it matter how a fictional movie portrays forms of government? Either we like the movie or we don't. I believe that we all have an absolute right to be interested in whatever we wish to be interested in, which I think implies the right to not be interested in whatever we choose to not be interested in. I think people have some obligation to be aware of global issues that affect society at large – it's not right to be indifferent to war, genocide, the climate crisis, and so on. But I strongly defend the right to not care about the political subtext of the *Star Wars* movies. If you just like the light-sabre fights, it's fine with me. If you would rather talk about basketball, or rap music, or whatever, that's also your business.

That said, it can be fun to analyze the political subtext of films and television shows with your friends. Young viewers may have not realized that it's possible to discuss the *Star Wars* films in terms of their political subtext. Perhaps after reading my essay, some *Star Wars* fans will have a new way to enjoy the movies.

8. What are three ideas you would like young readers (and *Star Wars* viewers) to take away from your essay? Insofar as I had some ideas about the *Star Wars* films themselves, my essay will have to speak for itself. However, I hope the essay also shows how powerful it can be to discuss real-world issues through fictional universes. So, idea #1: Memorable fictional worlds can make it easier to discuss complex topics in the real world. Film narratives shape how people view and interpret their own lives, or the society in which they live.

Science fiction and fantasy can be particularly good for pondering political issues, because science fiction is one extra step removed from the real world. Films about, say, the Roman Empire raise questions of believability: when Ridley Scott made the *Gladiator* films, was his picture of the Roman Empire accurate? One Roman expert consulted for the film was apparently so unhappy with the film that he or she asked to be removed from the final credits. Such issues don't arise in science fiction worlds like the *Star Wars* universe: the director's vision stands or falls on its own. So idea #2 is that science fiction provides a particularly good way to think about political issues without being distracted by questions of accuracy.

At the same time, however, it's important to remember the limits of this sort of analysis. Films can make it easier to raise or discuss important issues, but the resolution of a film is not evidence for how issues ought to be resolved in the real world. The *Star Wars* universe is fictional, and might not be internally consistent; film directors cannot imagine the full complexity of an actual social problem. What fictional characters do to solve problems in a cinematic universe might not work in the real world. Lucas never aspired to hyper-realism, but even films aiming for accuracy suffer inevitable imperfections. So, my final idea #3 is that while thinking about films may help us discuss important issues, they don't provide reliable guidance for resolving those issues. If you are looking for help understanding a political issue, it's generally better to consult a historian than a film critic.

CHAPTER TWELVE

How We See 'The Other' in *Tintin*

The Role of Empire in One of Our Most Popular Comics
Emma Walker

The explorer Henry Stanley in the Congo.

Editor's Introduction

In 1879, King Leopold of Belgium hired a British explorer (Henry Stanley) to build a series of roads across the lower Congo River region of Africa, and in so doing open the region's wealth to the world. One hundred thirty-two years later, in 2011, a film about a Belgian boy named Tintin became a worldwide narrative, earning close to four hundred million dollars, earning a Golden Globe for Best Animated Feature Film, and the title of highest-grossing animated film in India's history. The adventures of Tintin, featuring such titles as *Tintin in the Congo* and *Tintin in Amerique*, remain some of the most popular European comics of the modern age. A three-story museum, with nine exhibition rooms and a café, is dedicated to the comic book's author.

What is the connection? How did the Belgian presence in sub-Saharan Africa spawn a story that would so dominate the global imagination a century later? As I often tell my students, you do not have to buy any of my 'empire' theory, but you do need to explain these stories, and what it is about them that endures so powerfully.

ABOUT THIS ESSAY

Emma Walker offers one answer in this revealing interview and original essay. Her viewpoint includes the idea that we see evidence in comics like Tintin of a dominant European narrative, "the romanticized and most crucially the false representation of Asia and the Middle East as subordinate." Her thesis is that comics in general and Tintin in particular are valuable resources for cultural study. In studying them, we learn a great deal about colonial assumptions. The Author analyzes the art and text of specific *Tintin* adventures closely to prove her argument. She applies the work of scholars before her, such as Homi Bhabha and Paul Mountfort, to illuminate how the comic book adventures depict a world of harsh hierarchies. While the Author writes with scholarly detail, there is much a general reader (like me) can gain from her careful writings.

The point in all this is not that the work is evil, but that imperial attitudes can hide just beneath the surface of even our favorite, innocent-seeming stories, often in surprising ways. In this aspect, *Tintin* is in good company – we will see future postings about the changing Other appearing widely in children's literature, from *Peter Pan* to *Harry Potter* to *Binti*, and in comics from *Terry and the Pirates* to *The Avengers*.

One of author Emma Walker's touchpoints is Edward Said, and a second is the important concept of 'the Other.' I recommend her article and interview as an introduction or platform to these two valuable ideas.

The museum dedicated to Tintin's creator, Belgian cartoonist George Remi (Hergé).

EDWARD SAID

The father of Orientalism, Edward Said is a scholar whom English teachers like me often refer to. His ideas about the stories we tell can be extremely useful to our students, especially because they spend so many hundreds of hours consuming narratives of all kinds. Said's premise is that literature can be seen as a battlefield, with a dominant culture interpreting a "captured" culture any way it pleases. We tell stories to help explain how our society interacts with the world – in this way, all stories are "political."

Here is one of his observations:

> *Every empire regularly tells itself and the world that it is unlike all other empires, and that it has a mission, certainly not to plunder and control, but to educate and liberate the peoples and places it rules directly or indirectly.*

Said's concept of Orientalism involves the often flawed lens through which Westerners view other cultures. An example is *The Arabian Nights*, told by a British author, featuring a romanticized Arabia that only exists in the mind of a Westerner. Students will find this a versatile idea – one that is applied to America's foreign policy as well as the depiction of characters like The Mandarin and Electro.

THE OTHER

Of the many concepts I throw at my tired students in our ongoing attempt to jolt them into critical thinking and writing, "the Other" is always popular.

Students see the usefulness of "the Other" right away because we all spend so much time reading, watching, and telling stories – and we all know that certain characters are dealt a bad hand. Certain characters are portrayed as one-dimensional. They do not get backgrounds, flashbacks, or human motivations, or sympathetic characteristics of any kind. In monster movies it is the monster, in cowboy movies it is the Apache, in film noir it is often the pretty (but deadly) *femme fatale*.

Finally, I urge readers with an interest in these ideas to check out two articles in this online magazine, Patricia Kerslake's provocative "Science Fiction and the Other" and Tabish Khair's look at horror and the Other. We each must develop our own theories of literature as we consume and interpret these many narratives.

Link: http://empirestudies.com/2019/09/26/how-we-see-the-other-in-tintin-2/

How We See 'The Other' in *Tintin* | 83

Milton Caniff's "Terry and the Pirates," another comic which plunged a Western protagonist into other cultures.

Interview with Emma Walker
September, 2019

1. What three ideas would you like a general reader to take away from your essay?

There are three main points that I would like the reader to take away from this essay. Firstly, I hope that the essay demonstrates that Hergé's stories should be used as a historical source. As a piece of popular culture that harbours imperialist sentiments, *The Adventures of Tintin* are an indispensable source, not only for the Belgian narratives of national identity, but for the wider European narratives of empire. Secondly, I would like the reader to gain an understanding as to just how fantastically rich comic books are for the cultural historian. During the 'cultural turn' of the late twentieth century, very little attention appears to have been paid to comics, yet they provide us with much more information than we first suspect. Not only does the subject matter explore how identities have been forged through class, gender and nation but the prints, the colours, the cost and general material culture of the comic book, give us an insight into the lives of those who engaged with them. Finally, I wish for the essay to provoke the reader's own thoughts regarding other literary sources which also reflect an imperial consciousness. *The Adventures of Tintin*, whilst predominantly Belgian in origin, have a reception that stretches much further than their own nation. In light of Edward Said's notion of *Orientalism*, Hergé's work should be given as much attention as other imperial texts, such as Kipling's *The White Man's Burden* or Conrad's *Heart of Darkness*.

2. Paul Gravett writes that America's caped superheroes don't go over well in Japan, and that "Japan's unlikely champions are mostly aliens and androids." Does each culture give rise to particular comic-book heroes and heroines?

Gravett's argument holds much validity, especially in light of the Tintin stories. Tintin as a character, very much embodies the West. For John Mackenzie, the heroes of imperialist literature were 'male, had good looks and physical strength, were of good breeding and associated themselves with aristocrats'. It is entirely possible to also see Tintin in this way; he is after all a white, physically strong male, who is au fait with members of the aristocracy. Tintin demonstrates elements of the white man's dominance; he is, to invoke the work of Nietzsche, an 'ubermensch'-like figure. The strong, heroic reporter allowed readers to buy into the dominant ideology of the empire and in this sense; Tintin is an allegory for western power. He is a manifestation of the archetypal Western hero, created by Western culture.

Peter Pan is one of many children's classics with imperial roots. Art by Mabel Lucie Pullman (circa 1929)

3. Can you recommend further reading -- other works for students or general readers who are new to this topic?

The further reading that surrounds this topic is incredibly vast and varied. I would first start by recommending that you read other examples of imperialist fiction, for instance Albert Camus' *L'etranger*, Joseph Conrad's *Heart of Darkness* or Jane Austen's *Mansfield Park*. Other examples of children's fiction include *On the World's Roof* by Douglas Duff. For those who want to further explore the empire on an academic level, I would highly recommended reading Benedict Anderson's *Imagined Communities*, John Mackenzie's *Imperialism and Popular Culture*, Kathryn Castle's *Britannia's Children* and Frantz Fanon's *Black Skin, White Masks*. The work of Catherine

Hall and Simon Potter may also be of interest here. For those who may wish to explore the historiography of comic books in more depth, then the work of Jason Dittmer and Denis Gifford is of note. Further reading directly related to Tintin, includes Harry Thompson's *Hergé and his Creation*, Tom McCarthy's *Tintin and the Secret of Literature* and Paul Mountfort's article entitled 'Yellow Skin, Black Hair, Careful Tintin! Hergé and Orientalism'. This article can be found in the Australasian Journal of Popular Culture.

4. Is *Tintin* best seen as a product of its times? Would it be the same if it were created in the 2000's?

Of course, like any primary source, one has to pay careful attention to the context and whilst *The Adventures of Tintin* remain popular today, when historically analysing them, one has to remember that they will always be a product of the twentieth century. As shown by some of the images included throughout this paper, it is clear to see why audiences of today perhaps wince, cringe or take a sharp intake of breath when faced with Hergé's work. Undoubtedly, had the comic been created in the 2000's, the lack of political correctness would have likely rendered them deeply unfashionable and unpopular. Yet, I feel it would be anachronistic to place the comics outside of the context that they were written in. The stories connote racial difference through stereotyped images of the empire. The characters offer the perfect opportunity to externalise the villain. They evidence the emergence of imperial nationalism and they represent an imperial world view made up of racial ideas. They are the product of an imperial context and must be seen as such.

> **Hergé's work should be given as much attention as other imperial texts, such as Kipling's *The White Man's Burden* or Conrad's *Heart of Darkness*.**

5. For students considering for the first time a critical context of their favorite comics, is labeling Tintin "colonial" simply a matter of political correct-ness, or is it something deeper?

I think to disregard Hergé's work as simply a matter of 'political correctness' would be doing a disservice to his stories. *The Adventures of Tintin* provide the historian with a specific cultural understanding of the empire; they are part of a larger structure of meaning. I think Hergé is much cleverer than we perhaps give him credit for. Particularly throughout *Tintin in the Congo*, Hergé's clear use of irony sees the roles between noble and savage reversed. Whilst Tintin shows the Congolese citizens the benefits of Western progress, he himself degenerates into a savage hunter. It is actually Tintin who becomes the savage; the most civilised character ironically becomes the most animalistic. Hergé sophisticatedly caricature's the Western presence in Africa, as one full of hypocrisy. Similarly, thorough his portrayal of the Thompson twins, Hergé actually satirises the falsehood of his stereotyped characters. Their often exaggerated and somewhat absurd outfits seek not to ridicule certain national identities, but instead mock the twin's lack of cultural awareness.

6. You mention 'Tintin in the Congo' as a clear example of 'Otherizing.' Does Herge's work change over the course of the Tintin run? Do his views change, or develop, over time?

I think particularly with *Tintin in the Congo*, the concept of 'othering' is made quite clear. The solid, black gradient used to depict the Congolese citizens as well as the binary oppositional language of 'black' and 'white man', creates a strict dichotomy between the two. However, contextually we must remember that Hergé never actually visited Africa; he only drew on a mass of newspaper and magazine cuttings, prospectuses lauding life in the colonial service and picture postcards galore. In his diaries, Hergé explains how he 'was fed on the prejudices of the bourgeois society into which [he] moved…it was 1930. [He] only knew things about these countries that people said at the time and [he] portrayed these Africans according to such criteria, in the purely paternalistic spirit which existed in Belgium'. However, after his fourth instalment, *Cigars of the Pharaoh*, it becomes clear that Hergé's work does begin to change; these binary distinctions become less clear. After meeting a promising sculpture student, Chang Chong-chen in 1934, Hergé came to appreciate the differences in foreign cultures. He discovered a fascination with Chinese poetry and writing and I think from *The Blue Lotus* onwards, we can begin to see a development in Herge's views. Prejudices are somewhat swept aside and drawings become less caricatured. As I state in the essay, characters in *The Blue Lotus* are dressed in entirely western clothing and are made identifiable with the western world.

> **Hergé is much cleverer than we perhaps give him credit for ... Hergé's clear use of irony sees the roles between noble and savage reversed.**

7. In her work 'Breaking Barriers: Moving Beyond Orientalism in Comics Studies,' Leah Misemer writes that "Orientalism, where manga are cast as the exoticized Other of American comic books, has been detrimental to the growth of comics in the U.S."

What does that mean? Does it apply at all to Tintin?

I think Misemer has a very valid point. In fact, during the 1950s, many of the Tintin comics were found to be deeply unpopular within America. The Golden Books publishing house removed any content of inter-racial mixing and drunkenness from the comics, as it was deemed inappropriate for American audiences. Between 1966 and 1979, the Tintin comics were dropped by Golden Books and taken on by Children's Digest. It was not long after 1979 that they were dropped for a second time and given to the Atlantic Monthly Press. Only six albums ever made it onto US soil and I think part of the reason why Tintin struggled to grasp an American audience, was due to issues surrounding translation. The publishers often used the British translation of the books, which included many words which were not known to the American people. However, another big reason behind America's lack of interest in Tintin also boils down to precisely what Misemer discusses. Hergé's fifteenth album, *Land of Black Gold* is still banned from the US today as it concerns itself with the issues of the oil crisis of the Middle-East, a topical issue where America is concerned. The work of Ziad

Bentahar has analysed the reoccurring misrepresentation of the east through a western perspective. The albums pose a variety of questions concerned with the dichotomy between western and eastern cultures and identities. During the 1950s, there was a certain degree of western ignorance towards Asian culture and I think that there is perhaps a level of embarrassment present, that has prevented the stories from really taking hold in America.

CHAPTER THIRTEEN
Imperialism in the "Tarzan" Franchise

Hidden Depths in a Story You Think You Know
Anna Kozak

Editor's Introduction

What we call "Tarzan" is a sprawling collection, or mini-industry, of stories. The original Edgar Rice Burroughs adventure novel, *Tarzan of the Apes*, was published in magazines (1912) and then as a novel (1914). Since then, twenty-five sequels have appeared, along with books by other authors, countless comics, two stage plays, fifty films and nine television series.

It becomes important to separate the original "Tarzan" narrative from its many retellings in order to consider the saga in depth. It is a literary property that is more complex than we sometimes credit it, if all we know are the movies. To understand "the jungle king" and why he is such an enduring character – and so controversial – we need to filter out the story's many themes and elements.

Tarzan and James Bond In a recent article published in The Guardian newspaper entitled "Why Tarzan Will Never Be Okay," cultural critic Dave Schilling compares Tarzan to the British literary hero, James Bond. Like Bond, Tarzan gives us a model or an approach to modern Western cultures encountering 'exotic' cultures: namely, the West dominates. In Bond's case, an aristocratic Imperial messenger invades Third World nations on a higher mission: to save Earth from greed, treachery and destruction. The Bond stories have been called "a consoling fantasy" for the fading British Empire. Tarzan ('Lord Greystoke,' also British, also an aristocrat) invades Africa and becomes monarch of all beasts and humans. When he weds Jane, "the white couple are cheered and paraded around by their happy, loving black pals." Both the Bond and the Tarzan franchises tell stories about white Europeans conquering the untamed wilderness. Any black characters are incidental.

The power of literacy Where Bond makes good use of a fantastic array of gizmo-weapons in his buccaneering, Tarzan uses one all-powerful weapon: literacy. He learns to read, and through that, how to communicate in several languages. The written word saves him, leveraging his escape from 'the dark night of ignorance toward the light of learning.' When Tarzan stumbles across his parents' shipwrecked library he gains the tool that will leverage his supremacy over Africa – reading. Young Tarzan's discovery of the English book in the 'wild and wordless wastes' of Africa that changes everything. From this point on, he moves from a victim of his environment to its master. One critic writes, "as much as Burroughs is preoccupied with Tarzan's apprenticeship with weaponry—spears, nooses, bow and arrow—he seems more concerned with arming his character with literacy: reading, writing, and inevitably, speaking first French and then English."

Preview In this wide-ranging article, scholar Anna Kozak surveys the landscape of Tarzan stories and Tarzan analysts and gives the reader insight as to how the past century has changed Tarzan. She takes a close look at Clayton, the villain, and the way he draws attention to English national identity. Specifically, the author points out the British were proud of their Imperialism while the Americans tried to hide theirs. "[[The Tarzan story]] negatively portrays Clayton's overt nationalism," she writes, "since America's imperial power towards the end of the twentieth century critiques the explicit notion of Empire." She notes "the novel's focus on the Anglo-American alliance between America and Britain and the later shift towards America's critique of Britain's explicit imperial rule."

Another important idea that Anna Kozak brings us is that Tarzan is ERB's response to powerful worries regarding freedom and masculinity in the Modern Age. Teddy Roosevelt famously fretted in *The Strenuous Life* that we are all becoming "the timid man, the lazy man, the man who distrusts his country, the over-civilized man, who has lost the great fighting, masterful virtues, over the harmful effects of over-civilization which the modern age brings us." Tarzan can be seen as the embodiment of the noble savage ideal, and his primitivism as the remedy for umbrella-carrying males caught in the civilization's system. A century after Tarzan's first appearance, we are learning the true dimensions of these concerns.

Link: http://empirestudies.com/2019/12/16/imperialism-in-the-tarzan-franchise/

Interview with Scholar Anna Kozak
September, 2019

Q. Your thesis is that, in the progression of Tarzan's depiction, we can see the shift in imperialism over the course of the 20th century. How are the two "imperialisms" different?

How has Disney in particular altered the Tarzan story? How does this reflect our view of ourselves?

A: When Burroughs's novel was published in 1914, the British Empire was at its peak and made sure the whole world knew about its military successes. Yet, after America's rise to imperialism in the postwar era, there was a shift towards obscuring militarization. America did not want its own citizens to know about its involvement in wars, such as the Vietnam War, because it could lead to civil unrest (and it did); however, the widespread commercialization of the television and other forms of global media after the Second World War made America's reach for global dominance impossible to hide. Thus, gaining control of the media became America's primary method for redirecting attention away from its own imperial rule. But just because imperialism does not explicitly rest on a text's surface does not mean that it is not there. In an age of global American imperialism that functions hegemonically—that is, it rules through consent rather than coercion—it is easy to forget that it is there. Reading Burroughs's novel for the first time after having already seen the Disney version of *Tarzan* in my childhood makes it all the more apparent that Disney attempts to elide, or even obscure, the story's connections to imperialism. Yet, it nevertheless permeates the atmosphere and presents itself in various unexpected ways, as I discuss in my essay.

Q: What is the least-appreciated aspect or character of the Tarzan story?

A: The villain, Clayton, is in my opinion the least-appreciated character in the Tarzan story, particularly because the Disney film depicts him as a one-dimensional supervillain, while Burroughs's novel portrays him in a much more complex and interesting way. The Disney film completely erases the familial connection between Tarzan and Clayton that is so significant to the novel. Not only is Clayton Tarzan's cousin who only possesses Tarzan's family estates (because Tarzan himself is not believed to be alive) to claim them, but he also is supposed to marry Tarzan's love interest, Jane. This makes it even more imperative that Tarzan enters the "civilized" world of America and discovers his identity as the true Lord Greystoke. This battle for inheritance is one of if not the most interesting aspect of the novel, and it is a disappointment to say the least that the Disney film does not include this. Perhaps Disney considered this question of inheritance to be too complicated for a children's film.

Q: Can we enjoy the Tarzan story, or is it tainted by assumptions of imperialism?
Should it be re-written to omit this? Is that fair?
A: Of course we can still enjoy the Tarzan story. Tarzan's connection to imperialism does not taint the story but rather makes it an important textual artifact that carries with it valuable historical and cultural knowledge. It is important to study works that deal with issues of imperialism and race, even if they do so in ways that may be considered as less culturally acceptable nowadays. With that being said, there is no reason why a contemporary adaptation of Tarzan shouldn't rewrite the story to alter the depictions of Africans in the novel, for instance. Nevertheless, I do believe that omitting Tarzan's references to Empire altogether would be a disservice to its value as a historical and cultural relic.

> **Seeing Africa as a wilderness rather than as a place with humans living in it casts it as an uncultivated land that allows colonizers to justify claiming it.**

Q: Is Tarzan a search for identity story, or a story about nature and nurture, or a colonial fable? If it is a colonial story, is The Black Panther an answer to it?
A: In many ways, Tarzan is a story about all of these topics, and it would be interesting to explore the text from all of these various perspectives. If we were

to specifically consider it to be a colonial story, then *The Black Panther* could certainly be one answer to it. Reformulating the colonial tale so that it foregrounds the perspective of the colonized is certainly something that has been done before *Black Panther*; for instance, it has been an ongoing trend in postcolonial literature. Yet, the recent unprecedented popularity of *The Black Panther* in 2018 marks a major milestone—it shows us that people are now turning to popular media not only for explicit references to Empire, but that they are also becoming increasingly interested in colonial tales that do not center on the white man, such as Tarzan.

Q: Some critics view the Tarzan stories as a corrective for lost masculinity. The restrictions of the modern era, as Teddy Roosevelt predicted, brought confusion to the traditional male role, and ERB filled a need for a clear male role model.

What is the male image today? Is it Adam Sandler? Do we need Tarzan again?

A: Well, I don't really see Adam Sandler as the representative of the ideal male image today, but I do see how my reluctance to view him as the contemporary male role model is perhaps indicative of a more widespread rejection of the "average Joe" archetype that has become popular in the media today. There has been a rise in discontent with the dissolution of traditional male roles since the mid-twentieth century, and this discontent has even inspired Men's Rights movements and the like. Yet, the call for a lost masculinity is also not entirely a modern phenomenon as it could also be seen as stemming from philosophical treatises such as Rousseau's *Emile* in the eighteenth century, which calls for a return to nature in the childhood education of male youth amidst growing industrialization. As an important touchstone for children's education and literature, Emile argues that male youth can only develop into the ideal of the strong "natural man" through a retreat into nature and away from what Rousseau saw as the corrupting influences of society. These so-called corrupting influences of society have been increasingly linked to the feminization of men after women's entrance into education and the workforce, which some see as threats to traditional gender roles. Therefore, Tarzan could certainly be the symbolic embodiment of Rousseau's ideal natural man. According to these standards, Tarzan was raised in an environment as natural as they come and as far away from civilization as possible, especially if we consider the Disney version, which casts him in a wilderness with no African people.

> **Tarzan ... is a corrective for lost masculinity.**

Q: What does Burroughs think about race? What does Disney think about race? How does Burroughs portray Africa in the novel? How does Disney?

A: While I don't necessarily have access to Burroughs's personal thoughts about race, I can see that his portrayal of Africa and Africans in his novel does not go much beyond what he describes as the "low and bestial brutishness of their appearance" (103). Burroughs is very much a product of his time, depicting Africans as inferior to Europeans, but it is difficult to fault him as an individual for being immersed in the racist colonial ideologies that were prevalent when he was alive. Yet, Disney does not offer a particularly strong alternative to Burroughs's depictions of race—it decides to avoid the mention of race altogether by erasing any representation of Africans. As I alluded to in my answer to the previous question, Disney's portrayal of Tarzan as an ape man who grows up without any contact with Africans perpetuates the wilderness myth. Seeing Africa as a wilderness rather than as a place with humans who were living in it casts it as an uncultivated land that allows colonizers to justify claiming it. Thus, both Burroughs and Disney don't provide particularly positive portrayals of race through their respective versions of the Tarzan story.

> **Gaining control of the media became America's primary method for redirecting attention away from its own imperial rule ...**

Q: *"We wish to escape not alone the narrow confines of city streets for the freedom of the wilderness, but the restrictions of man-made laws, and the inhibitions that society has placed on us. We like to picture ourselves as roaming free, the lords of ourselves and of our world, in other words, we would each like to be Tarzan. At least I would."* ERB

What would ERB say if he were alive today? Would the villains whom Tarzan faces be different if he were writing it today?

A: This quotation brings me back to the earlier question of Tarzan as a corrective for lost masculinity. While we do not necessarily have to revisit that topic again, I do want to emphasize that there is a connection between the sense of the loss of identity—whether it is masculinity or not—and the pushback against industrialization. As Burroughs suggests, laws produce restrictions and inhibitions, which cannot be said to have not existed before the industrial age but perhaps become more noticeable during moments of turbulent change that unsettles society as we know it. If Burroughs were still alive today, the villains that Tarzan faces would probably be less likely to resemble another individual. Tarzan would probably assume the role of some kind of vigilante (like Batman) or anarchist (like Tyler Durden in *Fight Club*) and fight against modern society itself.

Still from one of the early Tarzan films, with Elmo Lincoln.

CHAPTER FOURTEEN

Empire and Higher Education in Nnedi Okorafor's *Binti*

The Empire Writes Back: New Directions for the Fantasy Epic
Amanda Lagji

Wikimedia Commons

Editor's Introduction

"The Empire Writes Back" is a powerful concept. It is a phrase coined by Salman Rushdie in a magazine article and then expanded in a book of essays (edited by Bill Ashcroft, Gareth Griffiths, and Helen Tiffin). It refers to a vibrant and vast body of literature told from the viewpoint of 'the colonized.' If the 17th, 18th and 19th centuries saw the rise of European colonial empires, then the 20th saw the beginning of a "postcolonial" period, The rainbow-rich cultures of giant nations (India) as well as tiny island cultures (Trinidad) began to take back their language, and to tell narratives from their own viewpoints – not that of the colonizer's.

This is one context to keep in mind in considering the *Binti* books by Nnedi Okorafor. They represent a new wave of authors who works written in part as a reply to J.R.R. Tolkien – these are epic fantasies written from diverse new perspectives, in this case an African perspective. In its way, *Binti* -- as well as books like Tomi Adeyemi's *Children of Blood and Bone*, and earlier works *Shadowshaper* and *An Ember in the Ashes* -- is part of the "Empire Writes Back" movement. The 'conquered' cultures are now creating their own fictional worlds on a par with the worlds of European and American writers.

In this well-considered essay and interview, scholar Amanda Lagji explores one specific aspect of the *Binti* story, one that appears in other epic fantasies – schools and museum, and how they can act as agents of empire. Robert Heinlein features a boot camp for imperial space-warriors, *Harry Potter* has Hogworts, *Star Trek* has Starfleet Academy, and so on.

The Premise of *Binti* In the *Binti* narrative, a young woman is accepted into a prestigious intergalactic university, Oomza Uni. She is forced to run away from home to take this opportunity, and soon she finds that powerful forces oppose her. This begins Binti's quest, not only to find her own place in the universe, but also to reconcile new knowledge with the ancient traditions of her people.

If most of that sounds familiar, it is because almost any epic fantasy comes with certain conventions which readers expect – journey to discovery, wise old mentors (who often die in the second act), sidekicks, magical creatures and fantastic artifacts trips into the underground, foreshadowing and flashbacks, etc. These are all elements established by *The Lord of the Rings* saga, written by a scholar who mined mythology for many of these elements. What is new is the texture of the setting, the imagery, and the special kind of story points brought by a West African language. Here, the rules set up by the mostly Caucasian European (English, that is) epic fantasists are changed by an infusion of African motifs and themes.

Afrofuturism Authors like Samuel Delaney and Octavia Butler initiated a tradition of speculative fiction rooted in African culture, often called "Afrofuturism."

In his essay, "Afrofuturism, Science Fiction, and the Reinvention of African American Culture," scholar Myungsung Kim holds that this new wave of authors "appropriate devices from science fiction and fantasy in order to revise, interrogate, and re-examine historical events insufficiently treated by literary realism." This merger of technology and black culture has created disruptive approaches to fiction, recasting our collective stories with a very different emphasis. Certainly HBO's "Watchmen" fits this bill, using a science fiction premise to re-examine narratives from America's Civil Rights era.

Kimberly Wickham, in her excellent paper "Questing Feminism: Narrative Tensions and Magical Women in Modern Fantasy," reminds us that fantasy authors have long used the fantastical to express dissenting opinions." She continues:

> Works of Epic Fantasy often have the reputation of being formulaic, conservative works that simply replicate the same tired story lines and characters over and over. That many works of Epic Fantasy choose to replicate the patriarchal structures found in our world is disappointing, but it is not an inherent feature of the genre. Other possibilities exist.

These epic-fantasy conventions seem innocent enough, yet at a certain point they are corrosive, for what they omit; the lack of characters of color sends a powerful message. Writes Ebony Elizabeth Thomas in *The Dark Fantastic*:

> The implicit message that readers, hearers, and viewers of color receive as they read these texts is that we are the villains. We are the horde. We are the enemies.

There are ideas beneath all stories. A reader's job is to delve below the characters, dig up those ideas, and give them a good look.

Link: http://empirestudies.com/2019/12/16/empire-and-higher-education-in-nnedi-okorafors-binti/

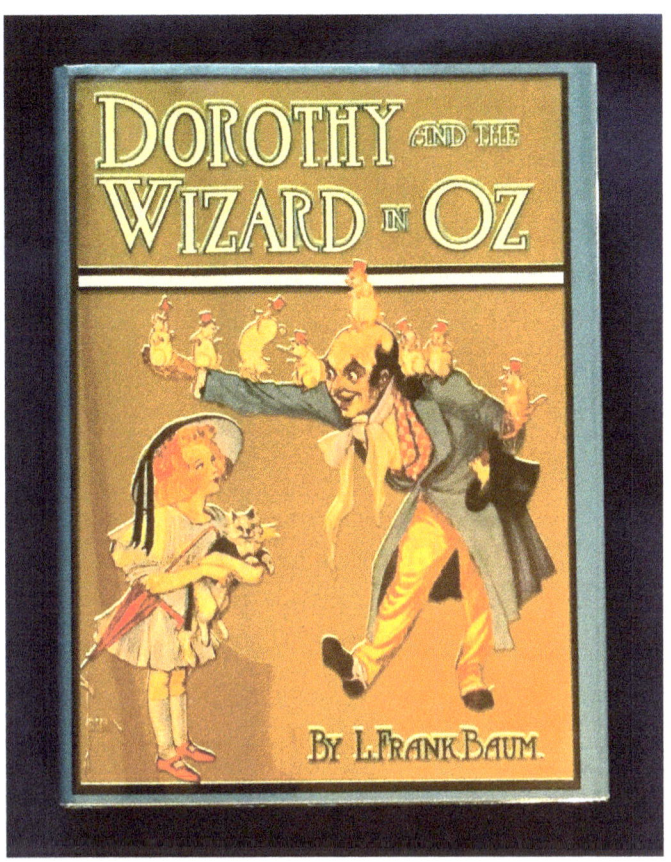

The 'Oz' novels served as pillars of conventional world-building fantasy.

Interview with Scholar Amanda Lagji
August 2019

1. What three ideas would you like readers to take away from your essay?

First, I hope readers begin to take the lens I use to analyze *Binti* and think about the spaces and institutions they inhabit, and consider how colonial or settler pasts are not distant, but are folded into the present. Second, I would challenge readers to think about the role of higher education and disciplines in privileging or discrediting ways of knowing; how do various disciplines define or value knowledge? And third, I would love for readers to seek out other Africanfuturist, Afro-futurist—or more generally, contemporary African—fiction.

2. Behind the interstellar travel and alien warfare, *Binti* and *Binti: Home* and *Binti: The Night Masquerade* are identifiable as coming-of-age stories. To what degree does the *Binti* saga build on coming-of-age stories before it, and to what degree is it completely new?

As a coming-of-age novella, *Binti* reminds me a lot of *Nervous Conditions*, by Tsitsi Dangarembga. The ending of *Binti* is a bit more hopeful for Binti's future at Oozma, but both texts share a concern about the ways that education—and especially, colonialist educations—require a debasement of self and disavowal of culture. Both authors, strikingly I think, write strong, young, female protagonists who are intrepid and reflective. And both Binti and Tambu (the protagonist in *Nervous Conditions*) feature in trilogies! Together, these fictional texts ask what the cost is of coming-of-age in the worlds they inhabit: what losses might they accrue to attain success or 'development' in the social contexts they find themselves? Rather than reconciling oneself with the world, these protagonists challenge their worlds to change to accommodate them. And I think that's a significant difference.

3. How do schools need to reckon with the legacies of empire? How might Nnedi Okorafor answer that question?

It is impossible to disentangle the legacies of empire from white supremacy; in the United States, we see a robust debate about reparations, about schools whose founders and patrons were slave owners, and about endowments made possible by chattel slavery and the genocide of Native Americans. The land schools occupy depended on the forced removal of Native Americans. Land acknowledgements begin a conversation, but they do not constitute or finish those conversations. The "how" will look different in different places, but it should address everything from the school's material and physical conditions of possibility (land, capital, labor, etc.) to the production of knowledge itself: Who do we read? Who do we cite? Whose stories and histories am I missing? What counts as knowledge? What are the implicit values of dominant worldviews?

Octavia Butler, pioneer author of Afrofuturism.'
Wikimedia Commons

4. Name an author or a work that Nnedi Okorafor's writing can be compared to (or contrasted with).

There are so many great Black science fiction writers—from Nalo Hopkinson to N.K. Jemisin to Samuel Delaney—but Octavia Butler's *Bloodchild and Other Stories* comes to mind to compare to Okorafor's *Binti*. Butler's themes are certainly more 'adult' than Okorafor's young adult fiction; in "Bloodchild," the eponymous story of the collection, a young human boy comes to terms with becoming a host for an alien species called the Tlic. The stories share an interest in exploring relationships between humans and others that does not reproduce the tropes of human discovery, conquering, and domination. One important difference between the two, however, is the authors' relationship to Afro-futurism. Whereas Butler is often read as a progenitor of the genre, characterized by "African American culture's appropriation of technology and SF imagery" (Mark Dery, 1994), Okorafor characterizes her own work as *Africanfuturist*. This distinction points to the centrality of African continent to her speculative fiction, which we can see in *Binti* as Okorafor draws inspiration from the Himba people of Namibia.

[See also her recent blog post: https://nnedi.blogspot.com/2019/10/africanfuturism-defined.html]

5. French President Macron recently ordered a report on 'repatriating' to Benin artifacts which French museums have been displaying for decades. They are seen to be stolen objects from colonial times.

Should we be re-thinking the museum displays we see on school trips? Can you cite legitimate museum displays and others which Steven Lubar might find offensive?

This is such a timely question, for many reasons! I'm currently teaching *Binti* in a course called 'Decolonial Futures,' in a unit that explores the decolonial imaginaries of contemporary science fiction. The unit that precedes it, however, is explicitly focused on museums, and we're reading about the Belgian Museum on Africa, Senegal's Museum of Black Civilisations, and the histories of Native American Museums and exhibits in the United States. We began the semester by viewing the documentary *Etched in Bone*, which follows the repatriation of stolen human remains from Gunbalanya, Aboriginal land in Australia. After the documentary, several students remarked that they hadn't ever thought about how artifacts and objects come to be museums, and that it made them curious and concerned. Museums whose collections consist of stolen artifacts are just some of the more obvious ways museum exhibits can reproduce colonial violence; Amy Lonetree's *Decolonizing Museums: Representing Native America in National and Tribal Museums* describes how exhibits that are not produced in collaboration with tribes or stewarded by tribes tend to rely on an object-based display that situates Native American life and culture in the past. In contrast, she describes a concept-based approach that calls for "[d]isplaying objects in ways that convey both their historic and their contemporary resonances" (22). In short, decolonizing museums will require the repatriation of artifacts, but that's just the lowest hanging fruit.

Sun Ra, purveyor of 'Afrofuturistic' music. Creative Commons.
Photo: Andy Newcombe.

6. Is *Binti* an American story of a Nigerian protagonist, or a Nigerian story, or a story with no nationality? If this had been written by an Indian author, or an Eskimo, would it be different?

I think one of the advantages of speculative fiction is to imagine a world where these questions don't exactly map on to the way our characters think about themselves and the world. Binti certainly has deep ties to her Himba people, culture, and history, but the novella isn't interested in whether that corresponds to a nation-state. So, in that sense, it's easy for me to say that this isn't a story of a Nigerian protagonist. Is it an American story, or a Nigeria story, or one without a nationality? I think American and Nigerian readers alike can see their worlds refracted in *Binti,* but I resist the notion that this story could be categorized along national lines. Okorafor herself has spoken at length in interviews about her own identification as "Naijamerican," a term that allows her to occupy the borders nationality erects between places and people. In that sense, I see her work occupying the same space.

7. For general readers new to literary criticism, what other works would you recommend?

Given the topic of my essay, decolonizing higher education, I would recommend **Ngũgĩ** wa Thiong'o's *Decolonising the Mind*, and especially the first chapter, "The Language of African Literature." **Ngũgĩ** is a writer of novels, plays, short stories, essay, and literary criticism, and he writes powerfully about the way language mediates one's relationship to culture, the environment, and history. For those new to African literatures, the first sections of the essay trace some of the debates African writers have been engaged in for decades: What qualifies as African literature? In contrast to the great Nigerian novelist Chinua Achebe, who famously defended his choice to write in English, **Ngũgĩ** asks, Why should a novelist "tak[e] from his mother-tongue to enrich other tongues?" (**Ngũgĩ** 8). I suggest starting with **Ngũgĩ** because, although not a work of literary criticism per se, I think it's helpful to read what writers have to say about their own writing.

In terms of literary criticism, I recommend Chinua Achebe's classic "An Image of Africa: Racism in Conrad's *Heart of Darkness*" for several reasons. First, students might have already read Conrad's novel or be familiar with its plot. Second, it's an incredibly compelling and persuasive reading of *Heart of Darkness*; each time I reread the essay, I find it difficult to disagree with Achebe's reading and interpretation of the text. Achebe addresses characterization, setting, the frame narration, and Conrad's own contemporary moment—all viable areas of literary criticism. It's great close-reading and a wonderful model of the work of literary criticism, but more than that, it's fundamentally changed the way Conrad's novel is read and taught.

Empire and Higher Education in Nnedi Okorafor's *Binti* | 107

Wikimedia Commons

CHAPTER FIFTEEN

Phillip Pullman, Polar Bears and the Real Arctic

How a Close Reading of History Matters to His Dark Materials
R.L. Shields

Explorer Robert McClure's The Investigator was trapped in ice throughout 1852. Authors like Phillip Pullman often use real-life episodes such as this one as the basis for his fiction.

Editor's Introduction

"Children's literature should be subjected to critical rigour as much as grown-up writing … Children's literature occupies a very different position from literature as a whole, largely because of two things: it's part of nurturing, in the anthropological sense, but it's also part of education."

– *Children's Laureate Michael Rosen*

Phillip Pullman, Polar Bears, and the Real Arctic

"Fantasy stories that are based on human history, even when significantly altering it, present certain challenges," writes R.L. Shields in her essay (below). The scholar takes the Phillip Pullman series *His Dark Materials* and *The Golden Compass* in particular as a case in point. In her close examination of the work, she reveals larger considerations.

His Dark Materials is a most ambitious epic trilogy (with two shorter books set in the same universe) with a large cast of characters, set in a complex fantasy world, depicted in the ambitious 2019 television series created by BBC and HBO.

The story's 11-year-old heroine, Lyra, travels through parallel worlds with a daemon and a truth-telling alethiometer (or 'golden compass'). All humans have a daemon and they represent a part of their personality, like alter-egos. Aided by armored polar bears called 'panserbjørne' (who may well be stand-ins for the Inuits), Lyra and her companions must deal with the mysterious Magisterium described as "a version of the Catholic Church that never ceded its power over Europe." *His Dark Materials* represents a significant achievement in modern young-adult fiction. "It breaks away dramatically from the tropes established by some of the giants of fantasy literature before Pullman," says Dr Dimitra Fimi, lecturer in Fantasy and Children's Literature at the University of Glasgow.

In this essay, scholar R. L. Shields looks at Pullman's fictional world to demonstrate that how we view the past can sometimes be through a lens that is warped. For example, the snow-bound sequences of *The Golden Compass* are based on historical accounts of Arctic explorers Martin Frobisher and Henry Hudson. Yet, she cautions, there are challenges in this re-telling of history:

> Phillip Pullman draws heavily on the British history of polar exploration as Victorians imagined or hoped it to be; his explorers are heroic, manly men who shape the landscape to their own will and beautiful women in impractical clothing who never look worse for wear. For the most part, references to cannibalism, scurvy, and other real indignities of Artic

exploration are left out of his version. There is little reference to frustrations and setbacks …

Next, she considers the role of 'sensitivity readers,' early readers who are meant to help fiction writers depict characters different from themselves carefully and considerately.

R.L. Shields uses these stepping stones to ask two larger questions:

1) Do we romance the past in the choice to resurrect it?
2) How does one balance nostalgia for some aspects of a historical period without seeming to approve of all?

These are questions we can apply with similar impact to epic fantasies like *Harry Potter*, with its many echoes of the British Empire, and *Dune*, a science-fiction work based on a feudal society in which noble houses control planetary fiefs. Closely tied to this consideration of romanticizing the past is our view of other civilizations, and how it has changed. Edward Said's concept of 'Orientalism,' of one culture can seek to capture another through narrative and art, is certainly a part of the discussion.

Shields ends her excellent essay with a warning for readers: "As Sampson writes, "Our responsibility as literary critics, however, is not to let the shadows of imperialism go unchallenged, even in acclaimed works of literature."

The wide-ranging interview which accompanies the article ropes in works from *Game of Thrones* to *Tripods* and authors from Zadie Smith to the poet Rick Barot in order to provide readers valuable context for *His Dark Materials*.

Link: http://empirestudies.com/2019/09/26/polar-bears-and-the-real-arctic/

John Collier's painting of the arctic explorer Henry Hudson, his son, and loyal crew set adrift.

Interview with R.L. Shields
September, 2019

1. What is a 'sensitivity reader'? Why are they needed now?

What would Mark Twain or Charles Dickens or Harper Lee think of them? What would a sensitivity reader think of these authors and their work?

I have an M.F.A. in creative writing and there is intense debate within that field related to representation and identity. Are we allowed to write outside our own experiences? Sensitivity readers are meant to help fiction writers depict characters who are different from themselves carefully and considerately. Usually, the sensitively reader shares aspects of identity with the character and can give writing advice based on lived experience.

A few years ago, I attended a lecture by the poet Rick Barot (https://rickbarot.com/) during which he told the story of a student of his (a woman of European descent) who wanted to write poems from the perspectives of Japanese people who had been held at Manzanar during World War II. His first reaction was to tell her stay away from this idea, but then he changed his mind and told her she could try it, but she needed to research the subject so thoroughly that no one would be able to say that she had been disrespectful. I think I agree with his advice. The answer is not to give up on writing outside your experience, but to always put your best effort into writing with care (perhaps with the help of a sensitivity reader). When it comes to something like Manzanar, it seems wrong to discourage conversation, even if the person bringing this historical moment to light is not the messenger you envisioned.

Author Francine Prose has an article (https://www.nybooks.com/daily/2017/11/01/the-problem-with-problematic/) about sensitivity readers in which she defends some of the authors you mention above. She thinks that the imaginative work of fiction is essential, as I also suggest in my article. Her focus, however, is on how imagining the lives of our contemporaries—even if our imagining is not always flawless from the perspective of a sensitivity reader—

helps us to emphasize with them and solve the problems of our current moment. Twain, Dickens, and Lee all critiqued the societies they lived within and used their stories to connect people across difference in order to build empathy and inspire social change.

2. Why should students care what lies beneath the surface of books and movies they enjoy?

Do these same ideas apply to the stories which students themselves tell?

The reason I think people should carefully examine the stories they love starts with my own childhood reading experiences. I remember thinking, when I was probably around ten years old, that it was too bad that there was only one kind of girl hero—most of the girls I read about seemed as if they were nearly the same person (red hair, fierce, good at traditionally boyish things), whereas the boys I read about could be heroic in all kinds of different ways. Some were shy, some were bold. Some fought with their hands, others with their words.

For example, I loved the *Tripods* books (by John Christopher) and they feature a trio of boys with very different abilities and traits who help each other escape from alien colonizers. I remember thinking that real-life girls must not be as interesting and complex as boys, or else there would be a larger variety of girls in books. This seems like a really bizarre conclusion to me now, but there were fewer children's books with female protagonists then. Needless to say, I'd much rather students learn to critique an author's choices than come to a conclusion like this one!

I differ a bit from some people, however, in that I think that critiquing a book does not mean that you have to stop liking it. I love many books that I also find offensive.

> **Most of the girls I read about seemed as if they were nearly the same person (red hair, fierce, good at traditionally boyish things), whereas the boys ... could be heroic in all kinds of different ways.**

And yes, the narratives we create do matter and we should think about how we tell our own stories. If my English-major perspective is not convincing, this recent article in the *Washington Post* explains how essential storytelling is for economists (and the public they are trying to speak to): https://www.washingtonpost.com/business/2019/10/19/worlds-top-economists-just-made-case-why-we-still-need-english-majors/

3. You write:

> *In some cases, there is an obvious pedagogical function of a return to the past—to emphasize how inhumane slavery is, or the unfairness of barring women from education—but, in many others, there seems to be at least some romancing of the past in the choice to resurrect it.*

What other literary properties "romance the past in the choice to resurrect it?"

Some of the most obvious examples of romancing the past appear in television shows or movies (many of them based on books) and *Game of Thrones* comes to mind right away. I'm going to get in trouble here because many people love the show (and/or the books), but I've had this issue with the story from the start: since this is clearly a fantastical version of the middle ages, why must it be dominated by white men? If you're going to invent ice zombies, why not gender equality as well? And, if we're really going to be historically accurate, why not take the model of medieval Iceland, where women mostly ran the farmsteads on their own and could sue for divorce?

> **If you're going to invent ice zombies, why not gender equality as well?**

Yes, there is a long list of exceptions to what I've just said about the series, though part of my problem is that they all seem like exceptions rather than the norm. Specifically, nearly all of the women in positions of power are one-of-a-kind. Brienne of Tarth is the only female knight we know of and Arya Stark seems to be fairly unique among assassins. Melisandre is a lonely priestess. Cersei Lannister, Daenerys Targaryen, and Sansa Stark only rise to positions of leadership after suffering years of abuse and powerlessness. Two of them are, arguably, made insane by their growing power (which does not seem to be an issue for the majority of men). Only one of them retains her position. Note, as well, that all of the women I have listed are not people of color (of the two most prominent women in this category, Missandei could possibly be called the power behind one of these thrones, but Ellaria Sand's storyline drops out of sight in the television series). In stories like this one, which is predominantly for the purpose of entertainment, I worry about what we find entertaining and how this scenario might speak to a nostalgia for a time when women had fewer legal rights and only a few exceptional women had power to direct their own lives.

Also, after the humid Missouri summer, I'm ready to join the Night's Watch and patrol the frozen north, so I hope they start recruiting women. Is winter coming soon?

Pullman's polar bear warriors are call 'panserbjørne.' Photo: Wikimedia Commons

4. Some English teachers (like me) tell their students that every poem, every story, every work of literature has an apparent conflict and a discovered one.

Does that apply to *The Golden Compass*? Does the reader discover an opposition that is completely different than the one we started with?

It would be difficult to pick just one apparent and one discovered conflict! Without giving away too much of the story of *His Dark Materials*, it's clear that questioning authority is a major apparent conflict. Various readers and critics have discovered conflicts between this clear message about disobeying authority and fighting for knowledge and some underlying ways in which the story actually upholds and reinforces particular types of authority and knowledge.

5. Edward Said suggests that almost every work of literature is, in its own way, political. Every poem, every play, every story sets forth a certain philosophy of the world in which there is a hierarchy; it can be used to further one nation or one culture over another.

Is *The Golden Compass* political? Is it a British story, seeking to culturally dominate another culture? How would it be different if it were written by a Japanese author, or an African author?

Yes, in a general sense, I think that *The Golden Compass* is definitely political. Pullman is saying that we should question authority, but he also might be implying, perhaps unintentionally, that certain elements of Britishness make Lyra particularly good at resisting and defying those in power. There are other characters who perform heroic acts and resist authority as well, so this is not true in every instance throughout the series.

It's hard to tell what these books would be like coming from a different perspective. I just saw Tarell Alvin McCraney's play *The Brothers Size* at the Steppenwolf Theater in Chicago. McCraney uses Yoruba myth and other techniques to tell a story about young men who have just been released from an American prison. In the play, it feels like McCraney is telling us that he needs to borrow another kind of imagining to explain how things are in the U.S. In a sense, he's saying that American mythologies are insufficient—that, instead of dominating the conversation, they need help, or even sometimes to be dominated by other stories.

Benjamin Jean Joseph Constant's "Arabian Nights" (circa 1899). An example of Orientalist art, a romanticized view of the East through Western eyes.

6. You write:

How does one balance nostalgia for some aspects of a historical period without seeming to approve of all?

What is the answer? Can young readers enjoy *The Jungle Book* **while at the same time disapproving of Kipling's jingoism?**

I'd like to answer this question by mentioning two current authors who I think do this well. Zadie Smith and Kazuo Ishiguro write with, against, and outside of the British literary tradition, often switching modes many times within one novel. Smith was born in the U.K. and has one Jamaican parent, and Ishiguro was born in Japan, but has lived in the U.K. for nearly all of his life. In both cases, it is very evident that they love some of the English literature that preceded their own, but also that they're very capable of inventing unique stories and techniques. Smith, particularly in White Teeth, creates a modern version of the panoramic novel that Charles Dickens and other earlier novelists pioneered. Ishiguro reimagines everything from Arthurian legends to Sherlock Holmes.

Their interactions with the literary past are far too complex to describe here, so I highly recommend reading their work to see how it unfolds.

> **American mythologies are insufficient ... instead of dominating the conversation, they need help, or even sometimes to be dominated by other stories.**

7. You end your essay with a warning for your readers:

As Sampson writes, "Our responsibility as literary critics, however, is not to let the shadows of imperialism go unchallenged, even in acclaimed works of literature"

Can you point out 'shadows of imperialism' in other recent films? *The Avengers*? *The Black Panther*?

I am a bit scared to weigh in on the *Black Panther* debate because it is so complicated, but I'll try. Many people applaud the way in which the film depicts an African society that has remained powerful and untouched by European colonialism. Many people argue that this kingdom (emphasis on "king") is too politically conservative in its structure and ideals. I can see the reasoning of both sides (and there are quite a few people who land somewhere in the middle of this debate, or somewhere else entirely, of course).

In the context of these reactions, the main thing that struck me when I was watching the film is that the story seems to go out of its way to undermine Erik Killmonger (played by Michael B. Jordan). Killmonger argues that the kingdom of Wakanda should use its superior technology to support a worldwide revolution of oppressed people. His viewpoints on reversing colonization might seem more reasonable if they weren't so bloody—if he wasn't named Killmonger and otherwise shown to be violent and power-seeking. I thought this choice of characterization showed some hesitance on the part of the filmmakers to seriously engage with a radical political discussions, or even just incorporate a more complex range of ideas within our current conversations about racism and reparation.

Pullman's work deals with religion and power in the fictional religious organization 'The Magisterium.' Pope Francis photo: Wikimedia Commons.

CHAPTER SIXTEEN
Pixar Gender, Pixar Rules

A Sampling of the Literature on Pixar

Wikimedia Commons

The full story of the history of Pixar is quite an adventure. Like every good story, it has its protagonists facing tall odds, believing in a vision, overcoming adversity and failure, moments of doubt, severely wrong turns taken, and in the end unthinkable success (more or less taking over Disney).

Here are four sample lit-crit treatments of Pixar from the large and growing body of Pixar scholarship.

AA. Gender in Pixar
by Tom Durwood

Jonathan Decker's recent dissertation "The Portrayal of Gender in Feature-Length Films of Pixar: A Content Analysis" was written for a Masters in Science degree. He has devised numerical values for cartoon portrayals and concludes what we have all suspected: Pixar represents a new and different generation of gender role models.

> **He concludes what we have all suspected: Pixar represents a new and different generation of gender role models.**

Decker starts by looking at traditional animated stories. He finds that mainstream movies have generally assumed an "androcentric" position – telling stories through the lens of male experience. Such stories tend to teach men to be aggressive and dominant, while encouraging women to be submissive and passive.

"Nowhere," Decker writes, "is the adherence to traditionalism more clearly displayed than in the animated features of Walt Disney Studios. Females in Disney films traditionally existed merely to exemplify beauty and virtue, to be rescued and romanced by males, and to serve as nurturing mothers." This, I think, is not so much any kind of conspiracy, or deliberate effort, but rather the dictates of the marketplace: beauty sells. "Those tales that have endured over the past 150 years," writes Decker, "are generally those that emphasize feminine beauty as a dominant theme, such as *Cinderella, Sleeping Beauty,* and *Snow White*."

Pixar has changed the landscape. While never drawing attention to it, Pixar has made films in which gender traits are much more equally distributed. From *Toy Story* to *Ratatouille, Monsters Inc* to *Finding Nemo, Wall-E* to *Cars,* Pixar has abandoned girls with long eyelashes in favor of girls with bows and arrows. In Decker's words, "Pixar writes strong and varied female characters, breaking free of the 'princess' confines of traditional Disney by portraying women as cowgirls, chefs, superheroes, and professionals." And this dissertation was written before *Brave*.

> **Pixar films show us a variety of character traits almost unseen in other children's media.**

For his dissertation, Decker coded specific physical and emotional traits in the characters. He gave numerical values to the appearance of lips and eyelashes, for instance, and characters who sport muscular versus slender builds in order to uncover what qualities make a male (hero and villain) and what qualities make a female.

Decker's results suggest that "Pixar promotes an altruistic, caring, and communal masculinity and provides strong, assertive, capable women in many roles. Pixar films show us a variety of character traits almost unseen in other children's media."

For any fan of Pixar with a tolerance for statistics, Decker's dissertation contains a wealth of observations, general and specific. Next time you watch an animated movie, you will begin to notice these subtle markers of gender, as I have since first reading Jonathan's paper.

> **While some gains were made in the 1990's, the 2000's have seen a return to celebrating "hard masculinity" and sexual objectification of females.**

BB. Family Roles in Pixar: An Excerpt from "Empowered Mothering"

by Suzan G. Brydon

Disney mothers have been consistently portrayed, when they are portrayed at all. Mothers in the last decade of the Disney repertoire remain nearly invisible, as matricide (or, more generously, mother absence) has long been a fairy tale action device and remains Disney's modus operandi for character development and audience bonding with the protagonist. Killing the parent (usually the mother) allows the young hero(ine) to mature through the precarious position it places the orphaned children in. There has been an historical dearth of mothers in Disney's animated fare and mothers with integral story roles in the last ten years remaining limited. **As of 2006, only 10 of Disney's 39 animated films with sustained plots featured living mothers**, and all of those mothers were either killed during the film or incapable "of protecting their offspring from harm"

> **In Finding Nemo, Pixar opened up space for a male character to mother ... In its stereotypes about gender, The Incredibles took a step backwards.**

Marlin was allowed to mother. Marlin shared food, groomed, nurtured, and taught. He tucked Nemo in, displayed emotions previously assigned on screen only to women, like fear and worry. In *Finding Nemo*: that for the first time in its discourse, Disney opened up space for a male character to mother (Brydon 2009). After complimenting Disney for stretching the boundaries of what mothering could look like and who could perform it, I ended my exploration by lamenting what appeared to have been a step backward in mothering representation with their 2004 release of *The Incredibles*.

Creative and progressive in some ways, *The Incredibles* (2004) also relied on long-standing stereotypes about gender and family roles, with father, Bob Parr/

Mr. Incredible, as a career-driven and hyper-masculine superhero focused on his breadwinning abilities and led astray by another woman, and mother, Helen/Elastigirl, as a stay at home mom who literally stretches herself thin to save her family and her marriage. In addition to their pre-verbal infant, they were joined by elementary-age son Dash Parr, whose super speed means he never sits still (epitomizing the modern ADHD-afflicted boy), and teen daughter Violet Parr, whose superpower was her ability to become invisible, especially around boys. Echoing some of my concerns, McMillan (2012) echoed many of my concerns in her analysis of the problems at the core of *The Incredibles*:

> While Bob gets his superhero groove back and Dash learns that sometimes you have to hold back in order to make the little people feel okay about themselves, Helen frets about the stability of the family and Violet gains enough confidence to ensure that she can wear more colorful clothes—a pink shirt, of course, because she's a girl—and talk to the cute boy in school.(par. 11)

Despite the impressive strength and abilities exhibited by the female superheroes in *The Incredibles*, ultimately the film emphasized the same old patriarchal, heteronormative structure we have seen in family films again and again.

The full text of Suzan G. Brydon's paper is available here: https://www.mdpi.com/2076-0760/7/11/215

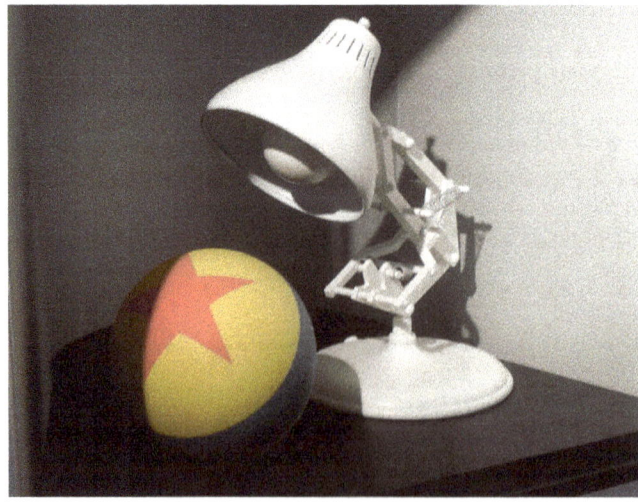

Wikimedia Commons

CC. Pixar Rules Part 1 (from a Pixar story artist)
by Emma Coats

A version of this article originally appeared on Aerogramme Writers' Studio. Follow Aerogramme Writers on Twitter @AWritersStudio.

These rules were originally tweeted by Emma Coats, Pixar's story artist. Number nine on the list—when you're stuck, make a list of what wouldn't happen next—is a great one and can apply to writers in all genres.

1. **You admire a character for trying** more than for their successes.

2. **Keep in mind what's interesting to you as an audience**, not what's fun to do as a writer. They can be very different.

3. Trying for theme is important, but you won't see what the story is actually about until you're at the end of it. Now rewrite.

4. Once upon a time there was ___. Every day, ___. One day ___. Because of that, ___. Because of that, ___. Until finally ___.

5. Simplify. Focus. Combine characters. Hop over detours. You'll feel like you're losing valuable stuff but it sets you free.

6 . What is your character good at, comfortable with? Throw the opposite at them. Challenge them. How do they deal?

7 . Come up with your ending before you figure out your middle. Endings are hard, get yours working up front.

8. Finish your story, let go even if it's not perfect. In an ideal world you have both, but move on. Do better next time.

9 . When you're stuck, make a list of what <u>wouldn't</u> happen next. Lots of times the material to get you unstuck will show up.

10. Pull apart the stories you like. What you like in them is a part of you; you've got to recognize it before you can use it.

11. Putting it on paper lets you start fixing it. If it stays in your head, a perfect idea, you'll never share it with anyone.

12. Discount the first thing that comes to mind—and the second, third, fourth and fifth. Get the obvious out of the way. Surprise yourself.

13. **Give your characters opinions.** Passive/malleable might seem likable to you as you write, but it's poison to the audience.

14. Why must you tell <u>this</u> story? What's the belief burning within you that your story feeds off of? That's the heart of it.

15. If you were your character, in this situation, how would you feel? Honesty lends credibility to unbelievable situations.

16. What are the stakes? Give us reason to root for the character. What happens if they don't succeed? Stack the odds against.

17. No work is ever wasted. If it's not working, let go and move on. It'll come back around to be useful later.

18. You have to know yourself: the difference between doing your best and fussing. Story is testing, not refining.

19. Coincidences to get characters into trouble are great; coincidences to get them out of it are cheating.

20. Exercise: Take the building blocks of a movie you dislike. How do you rearrange them into what you do like?

21. You must identify with your situation and/or characters; you can't just write "cool." What would make <u>you</u> act that way?

22. What's the essence of your story? The most economical telling of it? If you know that, you can build out from there.

DD. Pixar Rules Part 2 (from a sharp-eyed observer)

Kyle Munkittrick, writing in *Discover Magazine* ("The Hidden Message in Pixar Films," May 2011), postulates three rules of Pixar. Here is his explanation:

There are certain rules in Pixar movies that make things far more interesting than the average Disney fairy tale. **The first is that there is no** *magic*. No problems are caused or fixed by the wave of a wand. **Second, every Pixar film happens in the world of human beings** (see why I excluded *Cars*? It's ridiculous and out of character for Pixar). Even in films like a *A Bug's Life* and *Finding Nemo*, in which humans only exist as backdrops for the action, humanity's presence in the story is essential. The first two rules are pretty direct: the universe Pixar's characters inhabit is non-magical and co-inhabited by humans.

The third rule is that at least one main character is an intelligent being that isn't a human. This rule is a bit complex, so let's flesh it out. There are two types human roles in Pixar films. The first is Human as Villain. In films like the *Toy Story 1, 2, & 3*, *A Bug's Life*, and *Finding Nemo*, the protagonists are all non-human. Ancillary characters like Sid, the Collector, and Darla are not main characters. A more accurate description would be that they are pieces of the environment and, on occasion, playing the role of supporting antagonist. The second type of Pixar film is Human as Partner. In these films, the main character befriends a human being as part of the hero's journey: Remy, Colette, and Linguini; WALL-E, EVE, Mary and John; Sully, Mike, and Boo; Russell, Carl, Kevin and Dug. These are the heroic teams of their respective films.

> **The first Rule of Pixar is that there is no magic. No problems are caused or fixed by the wave of a wand.**

In each Pixar film, at least one member of the team is human and at least one member is not human but possesses human levels of intelligence.

Author Munkittrick goes on to explain his very specific theory about Pixar's message, having to do with mistrusting the future. The new is seen as dangerous and therefore feared. In so many Pixar movies, he argues, non-human sentient beings seek out human rebels. A team is formed when the mutual outsiders recognize a shared sense of purpose. Together, they overcome the high cost of non-conformity. The benefits for humanity are tremendous in every case where non-human characters are treated with respect.

Wikimedia Commons

CHAPTER SEVENTEEN
Philosophy in Comics

Discovering Socrates in the Comics
by Tom Durwood

The rationalist Spinoza and 'Owlgirl.' Both images: Wikimedia Commons

Although these outlandish figures in their capes, masks, and tights … are often dismissed as juvenile amusements, they really are profound metaphors for different approaches to shaping one's character.

-- *Travis Smith*

Save for a smattering of nonwhite characters (and nonwhite creators), these books and these iconic characters are still very much white supremacist dreams of the master race.

-- *Alan Moore*

The world of caped super-powered heroes is not exempt from the controversies that swirl in other segments of children's literature – nor should it be. Comics are a subset of literature, and all literature deals in one way or another with the human condition. It is no surprise to find strains of philosophy in these widely varied stories. Complexity, subtlety and shades of gray have moved into comic-book narratives which were once only seen in primary colors.

Here are four opinions for you to consider.

1. Each Superhero Represents an Idea

Let us assign a school of thought to each superhero. This doesn't work, not really. But in its failure, we can find some interesting connections.

- Capitalism … Iron Man / Tony Stark, Bruce Wayne, Scrooge McDuck
- Existentialism … Dr. Strange, Silver Surfer
- Nationalism … Captain America
- Nihilism … The Joker, Galactus, The Comedian
- Colonialism … Tarzan, Asterix, Tintin, Curious George, Babar
- Afrofuturism … The Black Panther
- Zen Buddhism … Dr. Manhattan
- Relativity … The Flash, Agent Carter
- Libertarianism … Batman
- Social justice … Watchmen
- Prejudice and The Other … X-Men, the Thing
- Feminism … Wonder Woman
- Our Place in the Cosmos … The Fantastic Four
- Social Collectivism … Society of Green Lanterns
- Monarchy… Thor, The Inhumans
- The Cult of Fitness … Batroc the Leaper
- Rationalism … Reed Richards
- Absurdity, Dadaism … Deadpool
- American Exceptionalism … Sgt. Rock, The Rawhide Kid

The Black Widow does not seem to me to be truly Russian, so I will not tie her to the Soviet system in my chart. Solomon Kane dresses like a Puritan and has a fatalistic approach to life that reflects predestiny and Calvinism, but he is a pulp hero, so he remains off the list. Charlie Brown. Lucy and Snoopy have spawned a small library of books detailing the *Peanuts* philosophies, but I cannot place them with any single school of thought.

The self-doubting Spiderman is one of the more philosophical of heroes, constantly giving thought and consideration to what he is doing. Doubt is a powerful element of both faith and philosophy. A key characteristic of Spidey / Peter Parker is his questioning the nature of his own gifts and his place in the scheme of things. The Silver Surfer, who suffers inner turmoil at his role in destroying planets, even more so, also the Black Panther. The Siegel and Schuster Superman was among the least self-aware of heroes. While that has changed in recent Kal-El portrayals, Superman's origin story and historical context work against re-casting him as Hamlet.

2. Morality

Superheroes are natural philosophers. Every third adventure or so, they tend to set the compass, asking some version of the essential questions: *Why are we here? How, then, should we act?* Almost every superhero story calls for the hero or heroine to make a moral choice. An important factor in that moral choice becomes the hero's motivation. Do they fight for personal revenge (*The Punisher*) or for the greater good ('With great power comes great responsibility')? Captain America and Batman would give you two different answers to that question.

The villainous Sandman fights for his daughter, who is ill. Does a superhero's (or supervillain's) motivation matter? In his essay "Why Should Superheroes Be Good?" C. Stephen Evans writes that Peter Parker has to sacrifice a great deal of his personal happiness in order to fulfill his Spiderman duties, while Superman is fairly blithe on this aspect of his destiny. Do we like Spidey more than Superman because of that? Is the inner struggle more important than the outward combat? There seems to be a spectrum or arc of self-sacrifice, even self-loathing (the Silver Surfer, for one) among superheroes.

Wikimedia Commons

Most superheroes refuse to kill their enemies, thus allowing them to cause even more havoc in the future. That is moral, but it is smart? Another moral question: How much damage to an innocent city (in the inevitable battle spectacle) is justifiable?

An American philosopher named Michael Walzer has a theory of "just war" and "war justly fought." He would say that World War II was a just war for America, the stakes being true life or death, while the Vietnam War was not. He would say that the nuclear bomb is an unjust method of warfare, since it targets civilians, while the Abrams tank represents a just weapon of war, one matched by the enemy. There are corollaries or examples of this in comics. Superheroes have a moral code. Some fights – and some ways of fighting -- seem correct, while others do not. Is using Kryptonite fair? Should Robin carry a shotgun?

Listing Batman as 'Libertarian' is an understatement on my part. The caped crusader has spawned more books than any other superhero with his ventures into vigilante justice. Esther Inglis-Arkell, writing in Comics Alliance, writes about Batman in *The Dark Knight*:

Batman tortures an incarcerated Joker to get information. It's shown as a moral digression, one which is echoed later in the film when Lucius Fox leaves Wayne Enterprises after finding out about a covert surveillance program. But in the comics, Batman has been torturing people to get information out of them for decades.

She raises other Batman-related moral issues regarding invasion of privacy, the balance of security and liberty, and the morality of training a child (Robin) to do deadly combat with armed criminals.

Watchmen, a comic book property which is a favorite among philosophers, sets out to destroy the conventional moral world of superheroes. Rorschach has clear black and white moral ideals (like Steve Ditko's Mr. A before him) while Night Owl can tolerate shades of gray. The Comedian lives to erase all moral boundaries, and Ozymandias seems to exist on a plane above them, considering his extremely harsh 'greater good' actions.

The philosopher Jean-Paul Sartre, whose existentialist views are reflected in comics like 'The Watchmen.' Wikimedia Commons. Photo: Moshe Milner

3. All Superpowers are Not Equal

Invisibility versus Flight For a 2001 radio feature on *This American Life*, writer John Hodgman conducted an informal survey in which he asks the age-old question: *Which is better: The power of flight or the power of invisibility?* He found that how you answer tells a lot about what kind of person you are.

What emerged from the debate over these two superpowers is the idea that invisibility is seen as a slightly sneaky, voyeuristic power, while flight is all about freedom and power. "Invisibility is a superpower for the villain inside us," writes theologian Brett Younger. "Invisibility leads to free movies, free plane trips and shoplifting."

In the end, Younger casts his vote for a third different superpower: the ability to stop time. Time, he argues, is what we value most.

A behavioral statistician named Joseph Folkman, writing in *Forbes* magazine, did his own survey and found that 72% of business leaders chose the ability to fly over being invisible (28%). "Those who choose the ability to fly are much more confident," Folkman concludes. "When you are flying, you are in the public light. Others notice you. You are at center stage."

Hodgman ends his consideration of flight versus invisibility with this thought: "At the heart of this decision, the question I really don't want to face, is this: *Who do you want to be, who is the person you hope to be, or the person you fear you actually are?*"

No matter which power people chose in the flight/invisibility survey, they never use it to fight crime.

Are some powers more meaningful or 'legitimate' than others? Some characters do not have a superpower so much as a skill – Batman, Hawkeye, and Green Arrow are among those 'superheroes' who are actually just physically gifted people who work out a lot and enjoy fighting crime.

If there is a caste system among superpowers, I am guessing Thor would be placed among the aristocracy and Sandman among the riff-raff. Paste-Pot Pete is one of my favorite Jack Kirby villains, but somehow I doubt he would sit at the head of the villains' table. His power of supergluing things to his advantage does not seem that impressive (no cape, either).

4. Socrates and Plato are Certainly Present in Comic Books

Philosophers Sarah Donovan and Nick Richardson see *The Avengers* as an entry point to the works of Plato. They compare Socrates to Captain America, pointing out that both men share a profound faith in the idea of justice. This guides all of their actions. "When people are just, it is because they believe in something divine and perfect." They contrast Cap and Socrates with Thrasymachus, a character from The Republic who believes we all act in self-interest. His motto might be, "We are only good when we think we will benefit from it. Donovan and Richardson pair Thrasymachus with Norman Osborn, Marvel's supervillain, the Green Goblin, whose situational ethics (and poor planning) place him in a dilemma he cannot escape. "Osborne does not believe in any sense of 'justice' beyond his own advantage," they conclude.

One of Plato's essential questions is his Theory of Being -- where humans locate in a universe of time and space. Plato believed that space was the arena in which things change, through time. Time moves through the realms of earth, fire, air and water. Einstein said that time and space somehow merge, that gravity can bend time, that time is not absolute, but relative to the observer. Time can vary depending on one's speed (through space). How do we work our way through all this? Comic books point the way.

Comic books provide a wealth of entry points into a consideration of time and space. Characters like The Flash, Captain America (and Agent Carter), the teleporting X-Man Nightcrawler, and of course Dr. Strange all deal directly with

Einsteinian notions of time and space. One of the top-grossing movies of all time, *Avengers: Endgame*, revolved around a central premise of time travel. Ditto *Dr. Strange*, in which the hero must stop time and re-thread it in a sort of loop, in order to defeat the dreaded Dormammu, Lord of Chaos. In *Superman: The Movie* (1979), Superman flies faster than light to go back in time and rescue Lois Lane before she is killed. In "The Flash" comics the super-speedster uses a cosmic treadmill to travel through time. Like Ted and Bill on their excellent adventures, like Hermione Granger in *Harry Potter* and Dr. Peabody with his "Way Back' Machine, The Flash moves freely through time, while he himself remains unchanged.

CHAPTER EIGHTEEN

Harry Potter: Last of the Breed

A Final Golden Age Work to Close the Door on High Empire Kid Lit
by Tom Durwood

A troll statue at the Atu Vanska park. Credit: Wikimedia Commons

Now that we have a bit of distance, we can place the seven-book *Harry Potter* collection in its truest context, or at least have some fun trying to do so. Brother to *Peter Pan,* cousin to *The Hobbit,* it is a work that both sums up and closes the door on the Golden Age of Kid Lit.

I made that up. It sounds pretty good, I think. Now let's see if it might be true.

Harry Potter and the Philosopher's Stone was unleashed on readers a generation ago, in June, 1997. Six subsequent novels and eight movies later, we can see the literary property more clearly for what it is: a member of the Golden Age family, along with *The Wind in the Willows, Winnie the Pooh*, Rudyard Kipling's *The Jungle Book, The Tale of Peter Rabbit, Alice's Adventures in Wonderland, The*

Adventures of Pinocchio, Peter Pan and *The Hobbit.* These books were written in what is often referred to as the Golden Age of Children's Literature. Not coincidentally, the authors were almost all British. The era also produced *The Secret Garden, Little Women* (American), *Treasure Island* and *Kidnapped,* the first pony book, *Black Beauty,* and many more.

The *Harry Potter* body of work is authentically High Empire, like its brethren, and serves as a sort of compendium of British literary traditions. We can also imagine that *Harry Potter* closes that particular door. It is the last of its breed allowing the audience to transition to the present phase of literature, Stage Four, or Falling Empire, a stage filled with equal parts dystopia, celebration of a complex world, and counter-imperial or corrective narratives. *Harry Potter* mirrors the end of empire, depicting as much in its own storyline. Let us trace Harry's lineage through Brit Lit and Brit Kid Lit and see where he stands.

The Potterverse is Built on a Foundation of British folklore.

Like J.R.R. Tolkien, J. K. Rowling is an author steeped in tradition. She studied classics at the University of Exeter, and her knowledge of mythology and folklore shows through in her writing. The powerful yet dim-witted **mountain troll** whom Hermione, Ron and Harry combat so fiercely in the dungeons comes straight from the Brothers Grimm and European folk tales, as do Rowling's **goblins**, **giants** (Hagrid, of course), **elves, werewolves,** and even the **hippogryph,** half-eagle, half-horse. **The Phoenix** is a mythological beast which can reincarnate itself. Dumbledore's pet Phoenix, Fawkes, sheds tears with healing properties, from which Harry benefits. Another Potter creature with ties to mythology (Greek, in this case) is **the multi-headed dog, Cerberus.** He guards the entrance to the Underworld in Greek myth, the entrance to the Chamber of Secrets in Hogwarts. The **centaurs** who live in the Forbidden Forest and the mer-people, although seen only briefly, first appeared in myth. The list of such magical creatures with origins in folklore goes on and on.

Conclusion: This shoe fits, but it does not count for much, since the other Golden Age works have little to do with fairy tales. Also, Rowling borrows from a wide range of mythology and folklore, not just British.

> **"Harry Potter" both sums up and closes the door on the Golden Age of Kid Lit. That sounds good; now let's see if it is true.**

Tom Brown's School Days

In his Victorian era adventure, "Tom Brown's Schooldays," author Thomas Hughes laid down the contours of a sub-genre of the Coming of Age story, the schooldays saga. In this, a lonely boy from a broken family arrives at an imposing boarding school with strange customs, meets a best friend, and overcomes an arrogant bully. With his pluck, his good nature and sense of fair play, the hero (Tom Brown or Harry Potter) shows up both his phony upperclassmen and his cruel teachers, all the while embodying the true spirit of the school (which had been falling into class corruption), saving it from itself. Think empire.

Conclusion: This shoe fits. *Booyah.*

J.R.R. Tolkien

Rowling's Dementors seem closely related to Tolkien's Dark Riders, or Nazgul, the same with Dumbledore and Gandalf (and Merlin, perhaps the original wizard). But extended parallels between the sagas of Hogwarts and Middle Earth don't hold up. For one, Tolkien's interest in how magic works is almost incidental to his story, while it is at the heart of *Harry Potter*, particularly in the character Hermione (who may be, along with Snape, the overshadowed heroes of the series). For two, Rowling's keen interest in plot and plot twist and closed-door murder-mystery-style scenarios has little in common with the long-striding accumulation of literary value in JRR's epic quest.

Harry is a member of the British Gothic family.

The Gothic tradition first emerged in the 18th century with such authors as Mary Shelley, Bram Stoker and Edgar Allan Poe (American). Characteristics of the Gothic novel include: death and decay, haunted castles, family curses, madness, melodrama and romance among gruesome terrors, and the regular appearance of ghosts (and monsters like vampires). In a typical Gothic story, an innocent young woman arrives at a remote mansion. Omens and visions foreshadow bad things. A ghost or monster appears so everyone knows a malevolent force is about to strike, usually as an act of revenge for her ancestor's twisted deeds. The clergy appears and is unable to stop it. In an overly dramatic climax, evil and passion are somehow connected. Buried secrets are finally revealed. Freed from her ancestral past, the heroine escapes with her handsome young love interest.

> **Literature ... does its best work in reminding us perpetually of the whole round of truth and balancing other and older ideas against the ideas to which we might for a moment be prone.**
>
> *-- GK Chesterton*

Both dark and intensely romantic, Gothic literature involves decadence. It is a little like imperial guilt – we have all this property and architecture and abundance, yet it is somehow corrupted. We cannot be happy, due to our ancestors' sins (is this starting to sound familiar?). Uncanny events lead us to the truth about our own tormented souls.

There are certainly Gothic elements in *Harry Potter* -- the omens and visions, for one. The irritating ghost Moaning Myrtle plays a pivotal role in *Chamber of Secrets*, for another, and the community of ghosts trapped in wall paintings serve as a chorus. The mysterious structure of Hogwarts itself is a semi-Gothic character, with its dungeon, secret chambers, and Escher staircases. As in Gothic tales, death and the thin boundary between life and death is very much present in Rowling's text -- Kipling's *Jungle Tales* and, oddly enough, *Peter Pan* being two other works which share this.

Conclusion: This shoe does not fit, despite the common elements of foreshadowing, ghosts and the trademark gables of Hogwarts. At heart, the Harry Potter story is not Gothic. Rather than madness and dark romance, Rowling's core values are teamwork, courage and devotion. Love wins. It is the characters' love for one another which uncovers true magic and defeats all the monsters. The teen dating at this boarding school is naïve and strictly young-adult, not the carnal, adult-bordering-on-obsessional that we find in such core Gothic works as *Dracula* and *Annabel Lee*. There is a strong rah-rah Quidditch component to *Goblet of Fire* and the other books that could never make its way into "The Masque of the Red Death."

Honorable Mentions

Wuthering Heights As we learn his whole backstory, we see that Severus Snape in the later Potter books comes to resemble Heathcliff, the brooding, dark hero of Emily Bronte's *Wuthering Heights*. This is a solitary, deeply devoted yet jealous, almost abusive, suitor who tragically breaks with the bright-eyed object of his love (Catherine Earnshaw, Lily Potter). These two glowering, black-haired figures lend both books a Gothic feel. We can see echoes of **George Orwell** and his opposite-talking ("War is Peace," "Freedom is Slavery") in the Potterverse Ministry of Magic ("Magic is Might"). **Agatha Christie** is a much more significant presence than Orwell in the Potter books, each of which is at heart a mystery. *Who is the Half-Blood Prince? Who saved Harry in 'The Prisoner of Azkaban'? Who opened the Chamber of Secrets?* Murderous doings in a civilized setting, with a closed cast of suspects (each with a hidden motive), misleading facades, an accumulation of clever clues -- these are all components of an Agatha Christie detective story. Like her literary aunt, Rowling loves narratives with secret passageways and dramatic reveals.

Wikimedia Commons

Jane Austen J.K. Rowling has told interviewers that "Emma" is one of her favorite books, and we can see why. While this 'novel of manners' aspect of the *Harry Potter* books is the hardest to capture – for me, at least – it is perhaps the most telling, in tying this work to its several Brit Lit influences. In her September, 2019 *Wall Street Journal* article, "Jane Austen Knows that Manners Make the Man," Paula Marantz Cohen writes that Austen's work "is now popular because of its eloquent portrayal of how politeness is tied to deeper morality." This idea, I think, has real resonance with the *Harry Potter* books.

> **As much as J. K. Rowling is driven by the books' intricate plotting ... it is her effortless presentation of the manners and conventions of the Potter world that readers love.**

As much as J. K. Rowling is driven by the story's intricate plotting, the movements of her giant cast of characters, and the many rules of magic, it is her effortless presentation of the manners and conventions of the Potter world that readers love. As in *Emma*, all of this correctness is tied to a deeper morality. It affirms a world order, and a polite one, unlike the chaotic, harsh, barely civilized world we live in today.

For example, when Dumbledore sets out to recruit retired Professor Slughorn, he must go about it in a very particular and indirect way, never letting on that he needs him. There are rules to the game, and if you abide by them, you win. When Harry flirts with a waitress in the underground station (in the movies, not the books), they both seem to know how this dance goes. Voldemort does not simply kill Harry in the graveyard after Cedric Diggory's death -- that would be bad form, and it would violate the hidden rules of the Great Game. Instead, he follows convention with a lengthy speech, thus allowing Harry and his ancestors time to regroup. Another example can be found in the character Dobby, who shows how lower-caste figures correctly (sacrificing their lives for the master) and incorrectly (self-flagellation) handle themselves. *Well played, Dobby.* The final example we have room to mention here is all the comedies of manners surrounding the Yule Ball – Hermione with Victor Krum, Ron with Lavender Brown, and Hagrid and his courtship of Madame Maxine. Heartbreak, misunderstanding, jealousy, misery and in the end joy. All of this could easily derive from the pages of a Jane Austen playbook.

Two Deliberate Omissions by Me

In my sad determination to prove my modest thesis, I am conveniently ignoring such non-British influences on *Harry Potter* as *Star Wars*. This despite lengthy evidence collated by clever readers like Scott Chitwood of theforce.net, who finds strong parallels between Obi-Wan and Dumbledore, The Force and Magic, owls and droids (both are messengers), magic wands and light-sabres. He cites many other convincing similarities. I suspect that, rather than borrowing from one another, these two sagas are similar because they both cleave so tightly to the detailed coming-of-age matrix outlined by such scholars as Otto Rank and Joseph Campbell.

I am also ignoring the influence of the German composer Richard **Wagner and his Ring Cycle**, since I don't really understand it.

Does Harry Potter belong in the Golden Age?

What qualities does Rowling share with Milne and Barrie and Grahame? Four elements, I think:

1) deep friendships at the heart of each story -- a family or substitute-family

2) literacy: a love of language and wordplay

3) a fully-realized imaginary world. Meticulously imagined, logically sound.

The fourth and possibly the most important ingredient is a High Empire Britishness, an imperial sensibility. The tea that Badger serves Toad and Mole was grown in India, the British colony, perhaps at one of the Chabua plantations, in upper Assam, courtesy of the Raj; that spotless train running from London to Hogwarts runs properly, without fail or falter, on-time, with snack trays making the rounds. Invisible servers fill the Hogwarts dining hall with an apparently endless supply of food; washer-women must be hidden in the dungeons, doing the laundry. The Gryffindor common-room carpets are Harshang Bidjars, from Persia, thank you very much. Life is good at the top of the pyramid. Smudge-faced working-class children in factories populate Dickens stories, not the hallways of Ravenclaw.

> **Rowling's most powerful story isn't the battle of good vs. evil. It's the long and lovely explanation of Voldemort's weakness and Harry's strength.**
>
> *-- Hank Green*

J.K. Rowling is a throwback, to British generations with an authentic high-empire sensibility. Her writing shares with *The Wind in the Willows* that British Empire quality of self-knowledge, or self-confidence, a deep, inclusive sense of where one stands in the landscape, so strong that it borders on predestination. Americans are looking for their place (*Little House on the Prairie*); the

British already know it; the French search for meaning (*The Little Prince*) among their places.

Included under High British Empire is the celebration of food and fine merchandise: Toad's excellent motor-car; the Hawthorne, Acacia and cherry wands of the Diagon Alley wand shop; Ratty's picnic lunch:

> 'What's inside it?' asked the Mole, wriggling with curiosity. 'There's cold chicken inside it,' replied the Rat briefly; *'coldtonguecoldhamcoldbeefpickledgherkinssaladfrenchrollscresssandwichespottedmeatgingerbeerlemonadesodawater*—-"O stop, stop,' cried the Mole in ecstacies: 'This is too much!' 'Do you really think so?' enquired the Rat seriously.

If the author had been Chinese, or Italian, or Hawaiian, would "Harry Potter" be a different narrative? A hundred times 'Yes.'

Codebreaking in WWII Wikimedia Commons

Sidebar: WWII motifs of spies, espionage, codebreaking

J.K. Rowling adds an extra vitamin of Britishness to her story by forging strong connections to World War II, more specifically the British experience of WWII. Such recurring motifs as the master spy (Snape), the turncoat (Marietta Edgecombe), the tortured prisoner (Charity Burbage), warring symmetrical hierarchies, codebreaking, hidden identities and love in desperate hours among the bombed ruins – all of these evoke familiar Churchillian scenarios, powerful images in the recent collective memory of British readers. Such elements and characters do not emerge from Russia's experience of World War II, nor America's, nor Japan's.

Sidebar: Harry is Definitely Not an American Hero

Each national culture and each age within that culture fashions a particular image of a hero. Sherlock Holmes belonged to the Age of Reason, breaking with a tradition of heroes who were simply powerful and brave. American schoolchildren learn about 'Honest Abe' Lincoln, Chinese textbooks might tell of Mao Zedong swimming the Yangtze, British youth all know the noble warrior King Arthur, while French fifth-graders can recite the story of peasant and martyr Jeanne D'Arc.

What kind of hero is Harry? Certainly not American, writes Ken Eckert, Associate *Professor* of *English* at Hanyang University:

> What I always find peculiar about the Harry Potter world is how Harry silently *endures* all the abuse he does, with a stiff upper lip, without complaining or rebelling.
>
> If 'Harry Potter' were set in the States, and somewhat also this is true for Canada, he wouldn't take all the crap he does from teachers, parents, and others. Americans love their heroes to be badasses who fight authority, and Harry wouldn't just grin when Snape cheats him on points, or there's some rule about what corridor he can walk down, or Hermione tells him about some school rule about the potion they need.
>
> When Harry saves the school *every time* from Hogwarts and still gets no thanks for it and gets yelled at by teachers, an American teenager would yell "F— you, you ingrates!" to them.
>
> Harry sneaks around rules, but he's no Holden Caulfield.

Added proof that Harry is not an American-based figure: the absence of fist-fighting, martial arts, gunplay and sword-fighting.

Conclusion

Our premise – that 'Harry Potter' is a legitimate member of the extended Golden Age as well as its gravedigger – is flawed. The Potter cycle may have more in common with adult Brit Lit – *Emma*, *Who Killed Roger Ackroyd* and *Dracula* -- than it does with *Winnie the Pooh*.

Madeleine L'Engle, author of *A Wrinkle in Time*, famously told a 2004 Newsweek interviewer that *Harry Potter* is "a nice story but there's nothing underneath it." The full question and answer is here:

> Have you read the Harry Potter books? I read one of them. It's a nice story but there's nothing underneath it. I don't want to be bothered with stuff where there's nothing underneath. Some people say, "Why do you read the Bible?" I say, "Because there's a lot of stuff underneath."

Firstly, comparing any contemporary work to the Bible is an awfully high bar. Secondly, we can now refute what was perhaps an offhand comment by Ms. L'Engle with a wealth of evidence: there is in fact a great deal of stuff underneath the nice *Harry Potter* story.

CHAPTER NINETEEN
A Revolution in Picture Books

A Sampling of Picture Book Scholarship
Tom Durwood

Wikimedia Commons

Introduction

In her recent dissertation, "Children's Literature Grows Up," Christina Phillips Mattson suggests that a revolution is brewing in Kid Lit, one that brings the complexity and sophistication of adult literature to children's books. While she meant this largely in the context of young-adult fiction, let's see if the premise holds when we consider books for younger readers as well, namely picture books. If we scour the excellent work of recent scholars, we can begin to assemble arguments for both sides of the thesis.

The Answer is Yes, a Revolution is Afoot

Comparing picture books from 1975 to today, you can definitely say there has been a revolution. Everything is different – the stories, the underlying themes, the artwork, the design – and especially the technology.

The aesthetics of picture books have been blown up by new media, world-changing events, and new social conventions. Mattson refers to "an emerging aesthetic and stylistic sophistication in recent works for children that confirms the existence of children's narratives that are equally complex, multifaceted, and worthy of the same kind of academic inquiry that is afforded to adult literature." Times change in each generation, and picture books change with them. This degree of radical change amounts to a revolution.

> **Technology has changed the landscape. The old conventions will not do.**

In their dissertation, "New Perspectives on Picture Books," scholars Lisa Ciecierski, James Nageldinger, William P. Bintz, and Sara D. Moore point to the new use of picture books to address a global community, and to do more than tell a simple story. The argument here is that texts for children have been leading us in new directions for some time, and rightly so. Sets of values have changed and expanded in a recent explosion of transnational storytelling. Our stories and depictions now reflect a wide world of possibilities and social practices. Young readers can step into the lives of Iroquois and Swahili and Eskimo peers, or a Japanese girl who folds paper into cranes – a widening of scope that amounts to a revolution from the times of almost exclusively English-speaking settings and characters.

Another sign of a revolution in Kid Lit is the books' willingness to stray into new narrative landscapes. More and more, picture books reflect our anxieties and concerns about wars, crime, global warming, epidemics and pandemics, street riots, and terrorism. Picture books have needed to venture into unsettling narratives and psychological landscapes to prepare young readers for the realities of life in the mid-21st Century.

These four scholars look also at the book format, or the 'post-modern' picture book, which highlights "design features such as strategic text placement, varied font sizes and dimensionality of illustrations." That is, the book no longer pretends to be a dimensional representation of a bunny in a field, a magical portal to another world. It's a *book*. A printed object. A picture book today admits and embraces its bookishness.

From "Dino Math: Sidd's Birthday," a storybook that teaches math. Empire Studies Press

Picture-book artwork is no longer limited to traditional representation.

Dr. Chi-Fen Emily Chen of The National Kaohsiung University has identified six categories of artwork in the post-modern picture book:

- A) Realism
- B) Cartoon Art
- C) Expressionism
- D) Impressionism
- E) Surrealism
- F) Folk Art

a list to which I might add Abstract Art, to cover such illustrators as Lane Smith and Leo Lionni. As to content, the postmodern book "is highly skeptical of explanations which claim to be valid for all group, cultures, traditions, or races, and instead focuses on the relative truths of each person." Wordless picture books like Ann Jonas' "Round Trip" place new challenges on young readers. Authors and illustrators might even share the processes by which they created the text and art. They need to try different strategies, since the picture book now contends with all manner of new media – not just movies and television, but streaming content, online games, digital resources. smartphones, and tablet apps.

> **Postmodernism is highly skeptical of explanations which claim to be valid for all groups, cultures, traditions, or races, and instead focuses on the relative truths of each person.**

Kathy G. Short, of the University of Arizona, points out that technology has changed the narrative territory. The old conventions will not do. She writes that "new technologies that encourage innovation in book format and design, have enticed new authors and illustrators, some of whom are transnational and thus move across global contexts, to provide a greater range of books for children."

The world is becoming more connected, more inclusive, more multifaceted, and so are the worlds depicted in Kid Lit. In her excellent *2020 Trends in Global Literature for Children and Adolescents,* Professor Short writes:

> In nonfiction, the dominant trend was in the number of biographies and memoirs with a focus on people from a much wider range of backgrounds than typically found in the past, such as memoirs of refugees from Somalia and Ethiopia and biographies of a female Chinese physicist, a Muslim world traveler, a Nicaraguan poet, a mathematician from

India and a Mexican chemist. In addition, collections of biographies about women from around the world were a strong focus in 2020.

Previously, if a non-Western culture was depicted, it was often in rural or small village contexts, with few urban depictions. Protagonists come from nuclear families.

Abused children appear in today's picture books. We see children of step-families, gay families, and foster families. Disabled children appear in today's picture books. Refugees and their difficult journeys appear in today's picture books, as well as some of the reasons behind their displacement from their homelands.

Children's literature has new uses, one being as a tool to teach mathematics and science, as in Rob Bolster's *100 Ways to Get to 100* and *Ada Twist, Scientist* (Beaty/Roberts). Picture books now serve as alternate teaching venues for such challenging topics as STEM, fluency, and social justice. Lastly, picture books have taken on the future, and regularly deal with coming trends like robotics, artificial intelligence, cloning, cyborg or hybrid life forms, genetic manipulation. A sub-genre had formed of eco-critical picture books, re-weaving the relationship between society and nature, technology and tradition – perhaps foreshadowing the next social revolutions.

From "The Illustrated Boatman's Daughter." Art: Serena Malyon

The Answer is No, No Revolution has Occurred

This argument postulates that the connection between the generation of "Blueberries for Sal" and "Parker Looks Up" is not a revolution, but rather a continuum. The current wave of talented authors and artists are still trying to explain the family and the world – it is just that families and the world have changed so much.

Exhibit One in the gallery of 'same thing, new version' is diversity: the representation of gender and race among picture books. It used to be terrible, and it still is terrible. The Anglo-American perspective still dominates. Males still dominate. As the study *Gender Stereotyping and Under-representation of Female Characters in 200 Popular Children's Picture Books: A Twenty-first Century Update* (Hamilton, Anderson, Broaddus and Young) demonstrates, not much has changed in fifty years. Sexism and racial bias in picture books are persistent.

> **The Anglo-American perspective still dominates. Males still dominate.**

No revolution here. The gender stereotyping and under-representation of girls and women in children's picture books in the past has not been corrected. Similarly, the percentage of characters of color appearing in picture books has remained unusually small. As Professor Short puts it, "The continued lack of diversity in children's literature is devastating for children as readers, many of whom rarely see their lives and cultural identities within a book."

In a chapter of their smart, provocative book, "New World Orders in Contemporary Children's Literature," scholars Clare Bradford, Kerry Mallan, John Stephens and Robyn McCallum refer to picture books as an important way to show transformations of global society. It is the job of picture books to show young readers how the world is changing: all this innovation is part of the fundamental mission, and not a new directive.

As early as 1962, illustrators like Ezra Jack Keats and Eric Carle were already experimenting with trick designs and flatness, figures and patterns. The new generation is following in the same tradition of experimentation. For all the talk about post-modernism, a book is still a book. Bold layouts, expressionist art, and wordless stories-- these are innovations, not re-inventions of the form.

As to the new and powerful themes we find in today's Kid Lit, if we look carefully, they were always present. In her dissertation "Dr. Seuss: The Man, the War, and the Work," Katy Anne Rice reminds us that powerful social themes have always been present in picture books. "Seuss managed to include very adult themes in his works that were presented in forms simple enough to be comprehended by children of all ages," she writes. "While using subjects as volatile as racism and the nuclear arms race, Dr. Seuss produced enjoyable children's books from which children and adults can learn."

Examples: More Traditional Picture Books

> *Goodnight Moon* (Brown)
> *The Giving Tree* (Silverstein)
> *Locomotive* (Floca)
> *The Owl and the Pussycat* (Lear/ Brett)
> *Madeline* (Bemelmans)
> *Harold and the Purple Crayon* (Johnson)
> *Green Eggs and Ham* (Suess)
> *Millions of Cats* (Gag)

Examples: Closer to Current Perspectives

> *The Girl Who Loved Wild Horses* (Goble)
> *Dreamers* (Morales)
> *When Sophie Gets Angry---Really, Really Angry* (Bang)
> *Ashanti to Zulu* (Musgrove/Dillon)
> *Where the Wild Things Are* (Sendak)
> *I Like Myself* (Beaumont)
> *My Princess Boy* (Kilodavis / DeSimone)
> *She Persisted Around the World: 13 Women who Changed History* (Clinton /Boiger)
> *Jumanji* (Van Allsburg)
> *Grandfather's Journey* (Say/Bunting)

Carlisle Indian Industrial School, PA (c. 1900). Photo credit: Wikimedia Commons. Once under-represented, groups like Native Americans today tell their own stories.

Conclusion

"The Theory of Children's Literature has for some time in a state of confusion," wrote Felicity Hughes in 1978. It still seems to be true, and there is no particular need for all scholars (or all readers, like you and me) to see things the same way.

My conclusion on this particular proposition is 'No.' There is no revolution in Kid Lit.

All literature strives to make sense of the world, and it changes as the world changes. Picture books have changed from the times of the Dick and Jane books, certainly, but the change has been more gradual than any sudden revolution. Picture books still feature art and story, a character with a problem to resolve, emotion to experience, and lessons learned along the way. They still fulfill their basic missions, a transfer of information from the real world to the reader, and a transfer of values from parent to child.

PART THREE

Lesson Plans

Nine Things to Know About Prof. Durwood's EN 210 Class

VALLEY FORGE MILITARY COLLEGE SPRING 2016

1. My job is to show you some of the great literature of the world. You will not like all of it. Some of it will seem "weird" or "boring." Your job is to overcome your initial alienation and see the literature for what it is – that is, in its context.

2. The Brockton miracle (constant writing) works. Practice, practice, practice. The Brockton miracle demonstrates that, with constant writing, your IQ and verbal skills shoot up, Listening to lectures—not so much.

This may be the last Literature course you ever take, so I have to be sure that ALL aspects of your writing game are sound.

3. Fake writers get punished. Many cadets like to talk a lot in class and then produce inferior essays. The essay is the whole point. With me, it's all about your effort. Do not wait until the night before to start work: that may have worked in the past, but it won't work any more.

When you give your presentation, we will all know how much research you have actually done. These presentations and essays almost grade themselves.

We will always review the building blocks of your essays together. I will circulate A papers so you have a very clear idea of what it takes to excel.

4. This – critical thinking and writing about literary structure and culture – is a very valuable skill. The marketplace rewards critical thinkers and effective writers. A recent study concludes that your salary is tied to the quality of your teachers.

I am so obsessed with your good reading and writing because I know it will give you a big advantage.

5. Each hour of this class costs you $120. Your parents are paying a ton of money for you to attend Valley Forge and take this demanding yet invaluable course.

If you want to doze through it and waste that money, it is your choice. DO NOT impede the class's progress since there are other cadets who want to get their money's worth. We only have 33 class meetings in which to transform each of you into critical thinking machines.

As you may know, any grade of C- or below does not transfer to your next college – that is, if you earn a C- it is like you never took this course. You and your parents will have to pay another $400-$1300 (depending on the fees at your next college) for you to take it again.

6. I don't care if you hate the assignments, or me. It's all about critical thinking and writing. Learn to read and research and think critically and write effectively and I will eventually stop bothering you.

7. Your most important work is done outside class. We have quizzes and mid-terms and final exams. Some cadets think everything is fine because the classes are lively, but your grade actually depends on the depth of your research.

While this is basically about research, it is really a double course: in addition to all the independent research you are doing, we also share your work with your peers in a vigorous presentation rotation.

8. The price for the free pretzels is your total engagement. I am working hard to give you all the writing and critical thinking you will need to be successful. If you do not do the assignments, I will have no regard for you. You will have no way to tell this is happening since I will still seem nice, but your grade will be very, very bad.

9. From now until the end of term (May 20), I am your writing coach. Your writing success in all areas of life is my goal. I am happy to help you not only with your assignments for this class but any other classes, as well as college essays, resumes, etc. (you will owe me, big-time).

tdurwood@vfmac.edu

WHAT IS THIS CLASS ALL ABOUT?

Our Mission

WHAT'S THE DEAL WITH ALL THIS WRITING?

A recent conducted by economists Raj Chetty and John N. Friedman of Harvard concludes that I am really important to you. The study found that:

-- Good teachers have a lasting positive effect on their students

-- A good teacher not only improves a child's test scores in the classroom, but also enhances his or her chances to attend college, earn more money and avoid teen pregnancy, according to a new seminal study.

 -- When a high value-added teacher joins a school, test scores rise immediately in the grade taught by that teacher; when a high VA teacher leaves, test scores fall.

Most importantly, the study discovered that "students assigned to higher VA teachers are more successful in many dimensions. They are more likely to attend college, earn higher salaries, live in better neighborhoods and save more for retirement. They are also less likely to have children as teenagers."

The effect of a good teacher on a child's life is monumental.

The Lasting Impact of Good Teachers, January 11 2012 http://www.cnn.com/2012/01/11/opinion/bennett-good-teachers/

AA. The Noble Hero

Aristotle said that "A man cannot become a hero until he can see the root of his own downfall." Do you think that is true? An Aristotelian tragic hero must possess specific characteristics, five of which are listed below:

1. **Nobility** (of a noble birth) or **wisdom** (by virtue of birth).
2. **Hamartia** (translated as flaw or error in judgment). Either a mistake in the character's actions or in his personality that leads to a downfall.
3. A reversal of fortune (**peripeteia**) brought about because of the hero's Hamartia.
4. The discovery or recognition that the reversal was brought about by the hero's own actions (**anagnorisis**)
5. The audience must feel pity and fear (fear that it could have been them!). Our empathy for the hero is sometimes called a **catharsis**, or healing process.

Initially, the noble or tragic hero should be neither better nor worse morally than normal people; he or she should be balanced in order to allow the audience to identify with him. This also introduces empathy, which is crucial in tragedy – we must feel for the heroine character. If she is perfect, the reader would not particularly care about what happens to her – Superman is a hero figure often cited as being too powerful, not flawed enough. Does the heroine get what she deserves ("poetic justice")? Does she earn her victory? It is important to strike a balance in the hero's character between strength and vulnerability, triumph and inner sadness.

Eventually the Aristotelian tragic hero dies a tragic death, having fallen from prosperity to adversity and having made an irreversible mistake. The hero must courageously face his or her death with honor.

YOUR ASSIGNMENT: Describe two Noble Heroes, one fictional and one real-life. How many of the attributes do they display? Do you think these matter? (500 words)

ANALYZE FAVORITE CHARACTERS
BB. Character

The achievement of great fiction is to create a character which the reader believes in, and wants to know about.

What makes for a memorable character in fiction? Why do you remember and want to keep reading about Katniss Everdeen, or Sherlock Holmes, or (in your case, Dawsey) Pikachu? What does a writer do to lend depth and likeability to a character?

Here are some traditional tools which writers use to create character:

-- a name with hidden meaning

-- the way they look physically

-- a distinctive physical trait (a limp, a scar, freckles) or piece of clothing

-- an endearing habit (humming, smoking a pipe, wiping off everything they touch)

-- what they wear or what they eat

-- their inner spirit

-- an unexpected way of speaking (stutter, using fancy words)

-- placing him or her in situations stacked against them, so we are rooting for them

-- an unusual or mysterious backstory that gives that character a special destiny

Many writers conceive of a character as clearly representing a single emotion or idea. A single action – often a moral choice -- can define the main character, or protagonist.

1. Name a character from a book or movie you like and name three specific aspects of the story that contribute to your liking the character. Explain why you like him or her so much. Is it what they wear? How they speak? For "Braveheart," for example, you might cite:

    a) his tragic loss (his young wife was killed by villains)
    b) his warm bond with fellow Scots soldiers, and
    c) his inspiring sacrifice for freedom.

Another character, Cinderella, might be compelling because of these elements:

    a) her happy attitude despite very unfair treatment by the stepsisters
    b) her affection for birds and animals
    c) her modesty as she attends the ball, and
    d) her terrible, unfair treatment at the hands of her step-mother (we always like the underdog).

200 words

2. Name three villains. How are they different? Are villains characters, or are they all just evil? Can they be "likeable"?

200 words

Optional bonus question: Name three sidekicks. Which is your favorite and why? How are they the same? How are they different? What do they contribute to the story? Why do so many of them die?

A KEY PIECE OF THE NARRATIVE
CC. Villains
ARE THERE CATEGORIES OF VILLAINS?
By Tom Durwood

Wikimedia Commons

How is an American villain different from a Russian villain, or a West African villain? What is "evil" to us? Why are some villains really powerful characters with deep grips on our imagination, and others just seem annoying? It is an important question, since villains can make or break a story: "Each film is only as good as its villain," declares film critic Roger Ebert. "Only a great villain can transform a good try into triumph." Here are four ideas on the subject:

a) Evil is either human and social, or cosmic. Professor Lee Quinby has considered these questions in depth, and delivers a powerful answer -- or certainly the framework of an extended answer -- in her dissertation, *Demurring to Doom: A Geopolitics of Prevailing*. She considers two "entrenched" categories of evil that have dominated American stories from the beginning: the first is cosmic or apocalyptic evil, and the second is human-driven evil, which is particular and specific. The *Terminator* movies feature apocalyptic evil, while a villain like Doctor Octopus in Spiderman represents one man's ambition and good intentions gone terribly bad. *Harry Potter* features both categories of villainy – Valdemort is apocalyptic evil, and the Minister of Magic's villainy seems more rooted in his personal vanity.

Both of these contending categories of evil, she argues, are powerfully delineated in Herman Melville's novel *Moby Dick*, especially in the character of Ahab, the villain of *Moby Dick*. Prof. Quinby also looks at President Franklin Roosevelt's portrayal of poverty as human-made and socially alterable. As the nation struggled against the Great Depression, Roosevelt was trying to motivate his countrymen – "We can fight this," he was telling us. "It is not our destiny to be defeated by poverty." Both Roosevelt and

Truman linked evil to social issues such as poverty, economic inequality, and the unchecked pursuit of profit.

On the other hand, terrorism is today often portrayed as apocalyptic – a cosmic force, something we cannot prevent or understand. Movies like *White House Down*, *Independence Day*, *Green Lantern*, and *War of the Worlds* feature evil like this – a force you cannot really understand (but must defeat). Certainly the Joker in *The Dark Knight* is like this -- he wants to bring general chaos to Gotham City for no rational reason. By contrast, the villain Bane in *The Dark Knight* Rises had a specific human story behind his villainy. Jack Torrance, the bad guy in Stephen King's *The Shining*, is an unlucky man controlled by a higher evil force.

b) American evil is often hedonism. Because of America's Puritanical streak, we tend to portray our villains as high-living creeps who transgress the work ethic. They are hedonistic – they enjoy material things way too much. They represent bad values. The *Die Hard* films, for example, feature villains who want to get ahead without working hard and playing by the rules – they want to cheat. That is why they are so despicable, and must be defeated at all costs. Corporate villains (*Robocop*) often fall into this category.

This is close to a class theory of *villains* – that bad guys are all upper-class, and represent the failed values of the rich, while heroes come from the working classes (the Green Goblin is wealthy, Peter Parker is middle-class).

Henchmen are minor villains and may not need a theory at all.

c) Each villain is simply the mirror image of its hero. Captain America is a strong smart hero (with no special powers) fighting for democracy, so the Red Skull is a strong smart Nazi (with no special powers) opposing him. That is why you can never switch villain – Lex Luthor does not fit against Luke Skywalker.

d) Any truly realistic story does not have a pure villain, only good characters who have made some bad decisions. An author named Ben Bova advises, in real life, "there are no villains cackling and rubbing their hands in glee as they contemplate their evil deeds. There are only people with problems, struggling to solve them." In *Les Miserables*, Jean Valjean turned to crime (he stole a loaf of bread) only so he could feed his family. Under this theory, only a weak story features a villain who is not at some point just like us.

YOUR ASSIGNMENT Please invent six categories of evil. Place at least three villains in each category, and briefly explain why you placed them there, and their relationship to the story's hero. What dos each villain represent? Which villains are strong character, which are weak? Who is the best of all the *Harry Potter* villains? Here are several villains you might consider:

Catwoman	The Sandman
Hannibal Lecter	Darth Vader
Dark Pikachu	Professor Moriarty
Professor Snape	The Joker
Predator	Bellatrix LeStrange
The Bad Terminator	Draco Malfoy

ELEMENTS OF HEROES
DD. Reversal of Fortune

"David Killing Goliath" painting by Pietro da Cortona (1596–1669)

In each hero story, an unexpected development – Oops! I slipped on a rock, or my best friend betrayed me, or sunlight blinded me for a second there, my weapon was just out of reach, I misread the magic map – brings about a terrible **reversal of fortune**. The hero is not only down, but way down -- further than she could have ever imagined. The worst part is that **she** or **he did not properly understand the scope of the original danger**. She is often chained up and powerless in a cave in a dark dimension that is worlds away from solving the real problem, and there exists no apparent hope for victory (… or is there?).

YOUR ASSIGNMENT Which hero went through the hardest times before miraculously turning things around? Who had the most dramatic and believable "reversal of fortune"? Please describe the reversal, whose fault it was, and how it gets resolved. What is the most dramatic reversal of fortune you know of in real life? Does any of this apply to you? (400 words)

IN-CLASS EXERCISE #4 ARE YOU ONE OF THESE?
EE. Heroes of Two Worlds
Due in Twenty Minutes

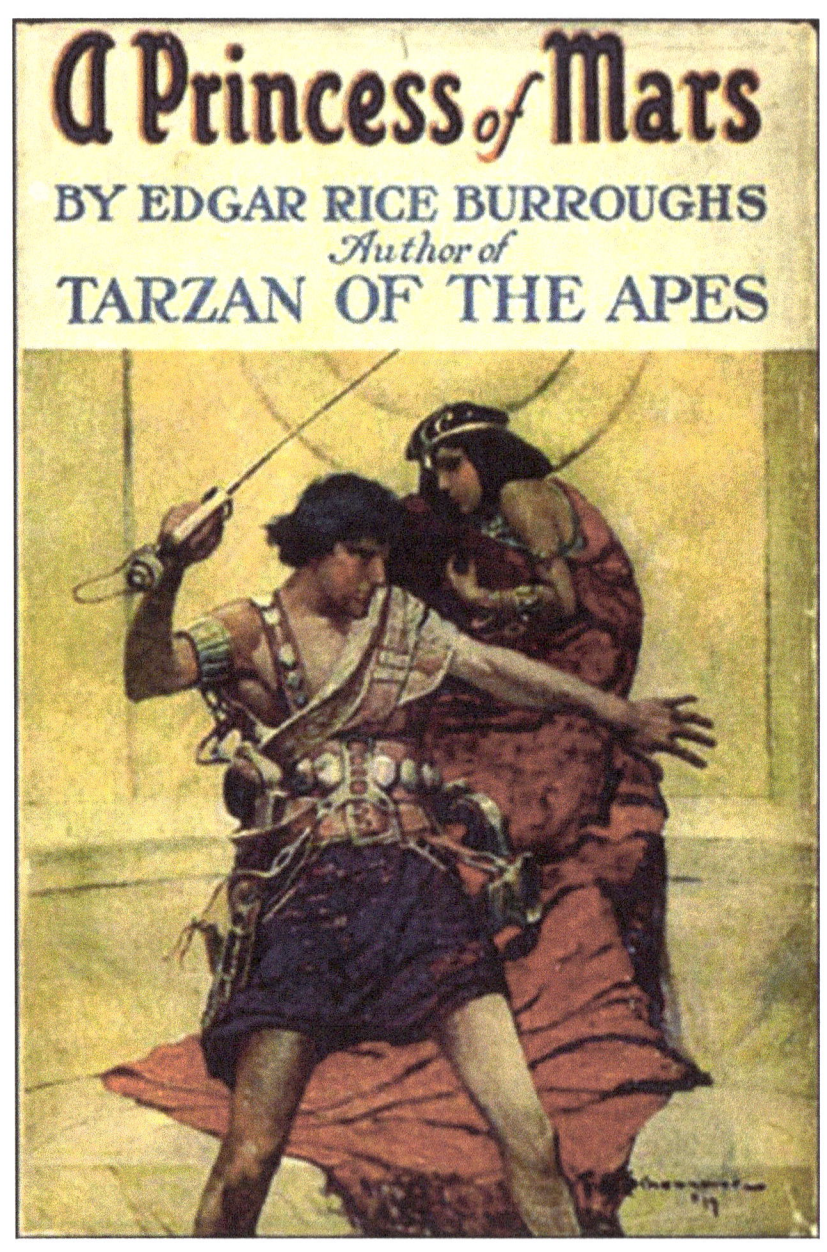

Many of the great heroes come from two worlds. Some even have two names and two identities. They are shaped by their original home and culture, and are sometimes lost in their new world. Yet the combination of the worlds within these heroes is precisely what gives them their great power as well as their great sadness:

- Superman = Kal El / Clark Kent
- Ariel, The Little Mermaid
- Blade the Vampire Hunter
- Lieut. Ripley (*Alien Three*)
- Liam Neeson in *Taken*
- Frodo Baggins in *Lord of the Rings*
- Bella in *Twilight* (third film only)
- Nicolas Cage as *Ghost Rider*

These heroes have two names, two identities. Do you? Does this belonging to two worlds make you stronger, or weaker? What special powers do you have because of this? What have you gained from each world that helps you in the other world?

Please write a one-page essay answering these questions. Draw specific comparisons between a hero from two worlds and yourself.

CRITICAL THINKING EXERCISE #7
FF. Open Letter to A Hero

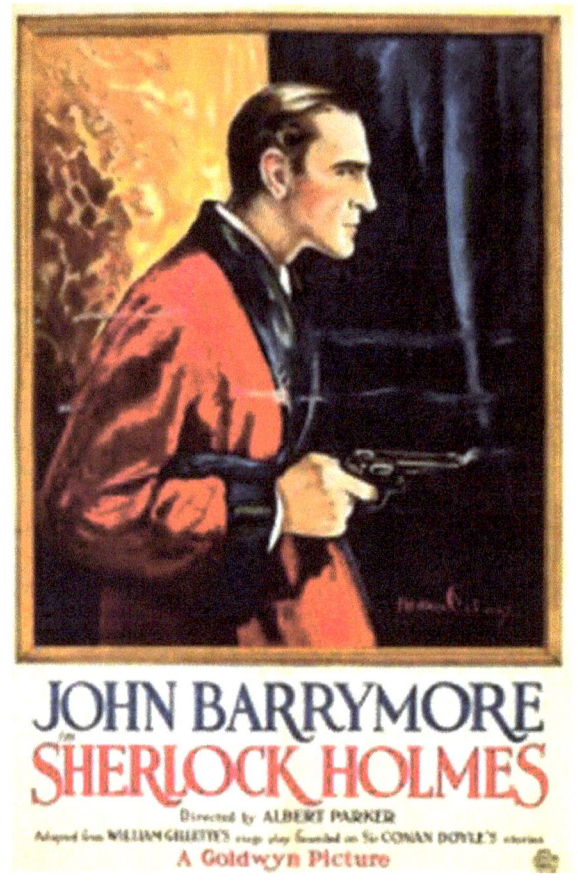

Wikimedia Commons

Attached please find an example of an "open letter" – these are letters you write to someone or something who generally cannot write back. They are usually funny (or at least really sarcastic).

Please write an open letter to a hero (or villain). You might ask about his or her feelings, or criticize how they have gone about their business, or inquire as to their core beliefs, etc. You could clear up any questions you have about their powers, why they did certain things in their epic story, their feelings about other characters in the story, if they have any regrets, how they came to be so mean, if they lived happily ever after or died young, that sort of thing.

Dear _____,

_____
_____
_____
_____
_____
_____
_____
_____
_____
_____
_____
_____
_____
_____
_____
_____
_____

Sincerely,

_____

SETTING
GG. Borderlands

Wikimedia Commons

Heroes often patrol a "borderlands" -- a place outside civilized society, on the remote frontiers -- where they a) gain valuable information or b) fight their epic encounters with evil. It is often far away from friendly place with families and schools and stores.

For example, modern-day heroes of the U.S. military patrol the "borderlands" or Afghanistan. Nicolas Cage in the motorcyclist-on-fire movie fought his demonic foes in a gigantic cemetery. Batman first encountered Ras-Al-Ghul in the far mountains of Tibet.

YOUR ASSIGNMENT (400 words)

Please list three heroes who patrolled a "borderland" and tell me where they fought their battles. Describe the borderland. Was the hero able to adapt to the borderland, and take advantage of the place to win his epic battle? Have you ever been to a borderland? What are America's borderlands?

LITERARY CRITICISM EXERCISE #19
HH. Man and Nature

You will see the recurring theme of man versus nature in dozens of forms in hundreds of poems, novels and movies. One form is man testing himself or herself against nature; a second is nature as a juxtaposition to (or a cure for) technology. Attached are several prose examples. Here are several more:

The Grey
Call of the Wild
Jurassic Park
Old Yeller
Dune
Into the Wild
Arachnophobia
The Lion King
The Perfect Storm

Jaws
Armageddon
The Jungle Book

Please create your own version of the conflict or interaction between man and nature. Please make it surprising.

It can be a short story featuring characters you invent.

It can be a continuation of another story.

It can be a poem (14 lines minimum) or 3 haikus or 3 cinquains.

DUE IN TWENTY MINUTES

II. VF EN HERO
Long Paper #1

Please compare two heroes – one from fiction and one from real life. You will explain them fully to someone who has never heard of these two, and then compare and contrast the two. Examples might be Gladiator and Barack Obama, or your mother and Sandra Bullock in one of her movies, or your uncle who served in the military and Blade.

What do they have in common? What was the heroic deed of each? What is the mission of each hero? What are his or her characteristics? Is he or she a noble (tragic) hero? Do they win or lose? Do they act for the common good, or for their own motives? When and where did they do their heroic deeds? In what society? Is there a connection between the heroic story and their society?

You will also give a 12-minute presentation to the class. You can use Power Point or film clips if you like.

750 words (three pages typed) minimum

First Draft due Monday Sept. 20 / Tuesday Sept 21

After hearing your fellow cadets' presentations, you will steal the best ideas from their presentations and use them to rewrite your own paper.

Revised final draft due Thursday Sept.30 / Friday Oct 1.

You have three highly capable assistants on this paper: Me, Prof. Zullo, and Dr. Baum-Brunner.

Be surprising. I have high expectations.

Sample Outline Hero Essay
Compare and Contrast

Introduction (for example): Despite their differences, these two hero figures share certain elements in common. While one is fictional and killed vampires in the subway (Blade) and the other served in

Vietnam (my uncle), both journeyed deep into strange territory to perform their heroic deeds. Both sacrificed for a greater cause. Both were betrayed by family members. Both recovered from their encounters with evil to live a long full life.

Hero #1: All about him or her

Hero #1: Beneath the image

Hero #2: All about him or her

Hero #2: Beneath the image

A Comparison: Points in common

A Comparison: Differences

To Me (the brilliant connection that only I have discovered):

Conclusion:

JJ. Pat Summitt and I Are Sick and Tired of Your Mediocre Efforts
YOU CAN DO MORE. MUCH MORE.

Tennessee basketball coach Pat Summitt routinely told her players that hard work is what counts. "This farm girl will never settle for mediocrity," she would tell her players. "Here's how I'm going to beat you. I'm going to outwork you."

That is what I am telling you now. *Work hard, cadets!* Take the next step in your evolution. Write the perfect essay.

YOUR ASSIGNMENT
Three Act Structure

Please break down two (2) novels or films into this three-act model. Do they fit the model? Do some have four acts? Two?

In a paragraph, tell us what happens in each act. How does this act end? Which is the most convincing act? Which is the weakest?

One and half pages minimum, typed.

Due _____

WRITING PROMPTS
KK. You and Literature

1. What are your favorite three books (or movies)? What is about the stories that you liked so much?

2. How would you characterize the following national literature:

Russian _____

German _____

Navaho _____

French _____

Japanese_____

Chinese _____

Zulu _____

3. A great story has the following elements (mark yes or no and explain)

   -- It's really sad

   -- It involves fate

   -- Love

   -- Excellent action (swordfighting, gunfighting, etc.)

   -- a plot twist

   -- characters that the reader cares about

   -- The bad guy loses big-time

   -- original characters

   -- good dialogue

   -- it resolves an exciting conflict

   -- it resolves a deep conflict, one that we almost can't explain

   -- it is set against war or some huge event

   -- the place and time = the fictional world

   -- other element

4. All societies like stories with happy endings.

True _____

False _____

ANALYZE FAVORITE CHARACTERS
LL. Character
PART II CHARACTER REVEALED

The best characters are more than what they appear to be. Name three characters, describe a) their surface appearance and then identify b) their "hidden" or revealed selves. What action or event reveals this true or inner character?

Example: Luke Skywalker

a) When we first meet him, he appears as a farm boy, a slightly whiny teenager stuck doing chores who would prefer to be driving speedy vehicles. Irritated by robots.

b) His inner self is a Jedi master, whose strength and purity of Force helps defeat the world-destroying evil of Darth Vader and Maul. Kind to robots.

Character #1: _____

a) _____

_____

_____

b) _____

_____

_____

_____

Character #2: _____

a) _____
_____
_____

b) _____
_____
_____
_____

Character #3: _____

a) _____
_____
_____

b) _____
_____
_____
_____

MM. Please Complete This Incredibly Easy Assignment, Cadet Kim

"Literature of Trauma" is literature which heals an old wound. Slavery, war, discrimination, bad childhoods – all these are elements that recur on literature as the author – and our society collectively – tries to retell the traumatic story until it becomes less painful to us.

The idea is that, unless we face the original trauma and understand it, we are doomed to always feel its pain – a little like facing your fears in a nightmare so you won't be scared any longer.

Alice Walker's novel *The Color Purple* is a famous example of retelling the story of slavery so it isn't so terribly painful – not just for Alice Walker, but for all of American society. Similarly, the "Rambo" movies retell the story of Vietnam (and this time we win). Do the *Die Hard* movies try to retell the 9/11 story so that this time we stop the terrorist attack?

Please write a poem or short story that "corrects" or resolves a trauma in your life. You can make it "masked" fiction – that is, one in which the actual scenario is represented as something completely different from the original. In this case, masked means disguised. For instance, *Aliens* is a masked fiction about Vietnam.

Minimum length (it can be as long as you want after this minimum is met). Poem = 14 lines / Story = 300 words

Remember:

Plot	Character development
Theme	Setting and descriptions
Imagery	pathos
Language / Dialogue	

Anagnorisis = moment of understanding

AN INCREDIBLY VALUABLE SKILL TO LEARN
NN. SUMMARY

Please summarize the attached article, "_____," in seven sentences.

1. _____

2. _____

3. _____

4. _____

5. _____

6. _____

7. _____

WRITING EXERCISE
OO. Reality Check

My ten-year goal:

_____
_____
_____
_____
_____
_____

My five-year goal:

_____
_____
_____
_____
_____
_____

My one-year goal:

_____
_____
_____
_____
_____
_____

My goal the rest of this semester:

_____
_____
_____
_____

I am a) lucky in this life b) unfairly treated c) seriously misunderstood and here is exactly why: _____
_____
_____
_____
_____
_____
_____
_____
_____

The biggest obstacle to my success here at this school and in life in general is this:

_____
_____
_____
_____

As a writer, I am really good – gifted, almost -- at this:

_____
_____
_____
_____
_____

I reluctantly admit I might need a little practice in this:

_____
_____
_____
_____

In this course I really hope the following is going to happen:

_____
_____
_____

CRITICAL THINKING ASSIGNMENT #44
PP. Female Characters and Difference Theory

Female characters are not just male characters with different bodies: they need to speak and act in ways that males do not. A researcher named Deborah Tannen has examined genders and finds the two very different. They are so different that you could almost call males and females two separate cultures: their speech reflects different worlds, and different underlying values.

The difference theory as postulated by Tannen is generally summarized into six or seven different categories, each of which pairs a contrasting use of language by males and use of language by females.

Status vs. support

Tannen states that, for men, the world is a competitive place in which conversation and speech are used to build status ["one up" or "one down"] whereas, for women, the world is a network of connections. That they use language to seek and offer support. In demonstrating this, Tannen uses the example of her husband and herself, who at one point had jobs in different cities. She remarks that when people commented on this, she interpreted it as being offers of sympathy or support. Her husband, on the other hand, took such comments as being criticism and attempts to put him down. Tannen remarks that this displays the different approaches that women and men take in terms of status and support.

Advice vs. understanding

Women seek comfort and sympathy for their problems, whilst men will seek a solution to the problem.

Information vs. feelings

Tannen states that men's conversation is message-oriented, based upon communicating information. For women, conversation is much more important for building relationships and strengthening social links.

Orders vs. proposals

Men will use direct imperatives ("close the door", "switch on the light") when speaking to others. Women encourage the use of superpolite forms, however ("let's", "would you mind if ...?").

Conflict vs. compromise

A woman is more likely to prevent fights and conflict by refusing to oppose or assert herself, even if it will not get her what she wants from the situation. Men are much more prepared to argue their preferences at the risk of conflict.

Independence vs. intimacy

Difference theory asserts that in general men favor independence, while women are more likely to seek intimacy. Tannen demonstrates this with the example of a husband making a decision without consulting his wife. She theorizes that he does so because he doesn't want to feel a loss of independence that would come from saying, "Let me consult this with my wife first." Women, on the other hand, like to demonstrate that they have to consult with their partner, as this is seen to be proof of the intimacy of the relationship. Tannen asserts that women, seeing the world as a network of connections and relationships, view intimacy as key to achieving consensus and avoiding the appearance of superiority, whereas men, who are more likely to view the world in terms of status, see independence as being key to establishing their status. Tannen also points out that both men and women seek independence and intimacy, but that men are more likely to be focused on the former, while women are more likely to focus on the latter.

Your Assignment

Please listen to conversations around you over the coming days and recreate one which you feel clearly illustrates the "difference" theory – that is, the difference between how men and women talk.

Comment on whether that conversation proves or disproves Deborah Tannen's "difference theory."

Minimum length: 250 words (1 page)

Due: Wednesday

UH-OH, INNER FLAWS
QQ. Poetry Part 5

Wikimedia Commons.

Empires are often brought down not by wars with outside enemies, but by inner flaws and moral corruption.

What does this short poem mean? Does it apply to you? To this school? To modern America?

> So in the Libyan fable it is told
> That once an eagle, stricken with a dart
> Said, when he saw the fashion of the shaft,
> "With our own feathers, not by others' hands,
> Are we now smitten."

Length: 250 words

Due: In twenty minutes

CRITICAL THINKING ACTIVITY #37
RR. "Beneath the Surface" Exercise

You are maturing as a writer. You are finding different styles in which to express yourself. You are transforming from a passive high-schooler to an active professional collegiate writer.

Now you want to make a habit of looking beneath the surface to see hidden structures and themes. The A grade lies in uncovering patterns and qualities that lurk beneath the appearance – of a poem, a battle, an election, a president, a character, a business.

1. Movie. On its surface, the popular smash hit *Avatar* is a science-fiction battle epic. It features a regiment of futuristic marines who get surprised when they invade a weird-looking, mostly blue-colored planet. Beneath this glossy surface, however, lie clear story structures and themes that are quite different. Here are two …

_____

_____

_____

_____

_____

Movie #2 (you choose). On it surface, _____ is about _____ and _____.

Beneath its _____ surface, however, this film is actually about _____

_____

_____

_____

_____

_____

2. Historical figure On the surface, _____ appears to be a _____ who

_____.

Beneath the surface, however, _____ is actually quite similar to _____

who _____

_____

_____

_____

_____.

3. Battle or War On its surface, the Battle/War of _____

_____

_____

However, as we look more closely beneath the surface, we can see _____

_____

_____

_____

4. Person you know

_____

_____

_____

_____

_____

_____

_____

_____ .

"If students are not being asked to read and write on a regular basis in their course work," Mr. Arum and Ms. Roksa write, "**it is hard to imagine how they will improve their capacity to master performance tasks ...** that involve critical thinking, complex reasoning, and writing."

-- David Glenn, in his review of "Academically Adrift," Chronicle of Higher Education,

Index

A

Adeyemi, Tomi 15, 99
Afrofuturism 15, 99, 103, 130
Agent Carter 130, 135
Alice in Wonderland 11, 24
Alien films
    Aliens 187
    Alien Three 173
aliens 49, 76, 84, 102, 104, 113
anagnorisis 33, 164, 187
Angelou, Maya 27, 43
An Image of Africa (Achebe) 106
Animal Farm (Orwell) 54, 60
Anne of Green Gables (Montgomery) 27
Arabian Nights (art)
    Constant, Benjamin Jean Joseph (1899) 117
    Parrish, Maxfield (1909) 57
Arabian Nights Entertainments (Burton) 10
Arabian Nights, The 82
Asterix 12, 54, 130
Avatar (film) 22, 49, 196
Avengers films 48, 49, 80, 118, 135, 136

B

Babar 12, 35, 54, 130
Babe (film) 47
Bambi (film) 66, 67
Barfield, Jonathan 61
Barot, Rick 110
Batman 23, 97, 130, 131, 132, 134, 176
Bechdel, Alison, and the Bechdel test 35
Bentahar, Ziad 89
Bibbiani, William 31
Billy Wilder's Ten Rules 45–47
Binti books 15
Black Panther character and film 94, 118, 130, 131
Blade Runner (film) 47
Blade the Vampire Hunter 173, 180
Bloodchild and Other Stories (Butler) 103
The Blue Lotus (Hergé) 88
Bock, Jerry 32
Bova, Ben 169
Brothers Grimm 10, 138
Brown, Alistair 15
Brydon, Suzan 123–125
A Bug's Life (film) 127
Burgess, Antony 33
Burroughs, Edgar Rice (ERB) 90, 91, 93–97
Burton, Richard 10
Bush, George W. 76
Butler, Octavia 99, 103

C

Cage, Nicolas 22, 173, 176
Cameron, James 49
Captain America 23, 49, 130, 131, 135, 169
Carrie (King) 25, 43
Cars (film) 121, 127
Catcher in the Rye (Salinger) 9, 25
The Cat in the Hat (Seuss) 12, 35
Cavallo, Francesca 36
Chang Chong-chen 88
character development
    Character Revealing Exercise 185
    devices used to build character 31–32
    dialogue, character conveyed through 33
    empire, effect on 53
    favorite characters, analyzing 165–166
    identity and 27
    in Billy Wilder's Rules 46
    in three-act model 38–40
    plot, role in 30
    sensitivity readers, advising on character depiction 110
    the hero as a balanced character 164
    the Other 82
    trauma of the lead character 42
character in literature and film
    comic book characters 134–136
    Disney characters 13
    female characters 35–37
    in Pixar films 122–128
    in Rick and Morty comic 76
    in Star Wars film characters 71, 78
    in Tarzan stories 90–97
    in works of epic fantasy 100
    Lion King characters 64–67
    Tintin stories, imperial context of characters in 84–88
    villains as characters 166, 167–170
Charlie and the Chocolate Factory (Dahl) 60
Chen, Dr. Chi-Fen Emily 150
Chetty, Raj 163
Children of Blood and Bone (Adeyemi) 15, 99

Christopher, John 113
Cinderella 41, 69, 121, 166
class 11, 41–43, 54, 66–67, 84, 169
Cleary, Beverly 12
climax 39, 40
A Clockwork Orange (Burgess) 33
Coats, Emma 125–126
coming-of-age (COA)
    adventure, initiation into adulthood through 19–20
    basic elements of 20–21
    examples in film and literature 9, 24–25
    in Binti books 102–103
    in British classics 11–12
    in family lore 8
    nature, positive and negative experiences with 44
Comparing Heroes essays 180
Conrad, Joseph 32, 84, 85, 106
crisis and resolution 39
Curious George 13, 54, 130

D

Dahl, Roald 60
Dambusters (film) 74
Dangarembga, Tsitsi 102
Dark Knight films 23, 132, 168
Decker, Jonathan 121–123
Decolonising the Mind (Ngũgĩ) 106
Decolonizing Museums (Lonetree) 105
Delaney, Samuel 99, 103
de Lauretis, Teresa 37
Demurring to Doom (Quinby) 168
denouement 40
Detrow, Scott 70
dialogue 33, 75
Dickens, Charles 41, 112, 117
Die Hard films 23, 169, 187
Disney
    caste system in Disney movies 66–68
    coming-of-age films, producing 25
    dead parent trope 68
    generational impact of Disney characters 13
    Lion King, message of fascism in 59
    Pixar as competition 120, 122, 127
    princess protagonists, success with 42
    Star Wars franchise, taking over 75
    Tarzan film adaptation 93–97
    traditionalism, upholding 121
Doctor Octopus 23, 168
Donovan, Sarah 135
dramatic premise 38
Dr. Seuss 12, 14, 155
Dr. Strange 130, 135

Dune (Herbert) 110–111, 178

E

Ebert, Roger 167
Elizabethtown (film) 35
Emile (Rousseau) 95
empire in literature
    American critique of empire 92
    American revolt against empire, as inspiring 48
    Black Panther, references to empire in 95
    "Empire Writes Back" movement 98–100
    essay question on empire and corruption 195
    four stages of empire 53–55
    Galactic Empire in Star Wars films 50, 70, 73–78
    Harry Potter and echoes of the British Empire 110
    Orientalism theory and 52
    Peter Pan, High Empire in 50, 80, 85
    Roman Empire in literature and film 50, 71, 73, 78
    schools, as carrying the legacy of empire 102
    Tarzan, empire reflected in 90–97
    Tintin, providing cultural understanding of empire 84, 87
Erik Killmonger 118
Etched in Bone (documentary) 104
Evans, C. Stephen 131
evil
    apocalyptic evil 23, 167–169
    as human, social or cosmic 168
    coming-of-age stories, as an element in 20
    essay question on 170
    hedonism as the American evil 168
    heroes, fighting against 22, 176, 181
    in Middle Earth 50
    in plot symmetry 30
exposition 38

F

fascism in film 59, 63, 68
Favilli, Elena 36
female characters
    animal protagonists, rarely depicted as female 34
    femme fatales 28, 82
    in coming-of-age novellas 102
    in difference theory 36
    in Disney films 121
    in Game of Thrones 114–115
    in picture books 154
    in Pixar productions 122, 124
    in Star Wars films 73
    Lotus Flower Woman 22
    "Mary Sue" type 35
Ferguson, Niall 52

Fiddler on the Roof (musical) 32
Fimi, Dimitra 109
Finding Nemo (film) 121, 123, 127
first culmination 39
Flood, Alison 35
Folkman, Joseph 134
Friedman, John N. 163
Frobisher, Martin 109
Frodo Baggins 40, 173

G

Game of Thrones (Martin) 13, 110, 114
Gandalf 39, 139
gender 34–37, 84, 95, 114, 120–126, 154
Gillard, Colleen 10, 12
Girl, Interrupted (Kaysen) 12
The Golden Compass (Pullman) 109–110, 116
Golding, William 53, 60
Grahame, Kenneth 11, 54
Gravett, Paul 84
Green Goblin 135, 169
Green Lantern (film) 23, 168

H

Hamlet character and film 47, 61, 64–65, 131
Harry Potter series
   Billy Wilder's Rules, applying 47
   coming-of-age narrative, exemplifying 24
   Hermione Granger in 36, 136, 138, 139, 143, 146
   High Empire and 54–55, 99, 110, 137–147
   political violence, raising the question of 77
   the Other in 80
   UK Parliament, evil government representing 71
   villany in 23, 60, 168, 170
   WWII London bombings, drawing from 48–49
Hassler-Forest, Dan 59–60, 63–68
Heart of Darkness (Conrad) 84, 85, 106
Heinlein, Robert 99
Hemingway, Ernest 32
Hergé, George Remi 81, 84–89
heroes
   American superheroes, Japan not favoring 84
   anagnorisis experiences 33
   as mirror image of villains 23, 169
   borderlands, heroes patrolling 22
   female sidekicks to male heroes 35
   girl heroes in children's literature 113
   Hermione Granger as hero of Harry Potter 36
   heroines in class-based fairy tales 42
   hero's journey aspect of Star Wars 74
   Hiroshima bombing, as influencing superhero movies 49
   in coming-of-age stories 19–24, 44
   in Pixar films 120, 123–125, 127
   in the three-act model 39
   morality of superheroes 131
   Noble Hero writing exercise 164
   Open Letter to a Hero assignment 174
   reversal of fortune, experiencing 171
   schools of thought, assigning to superheroes 130–131
   superpowers not required for 134
   two worlds, heroes as figures of 21, 172–173
Hinton, S.E. 13, 25, 41, 55
His Dark Materials series 44, 108–111
Hodgman, John 134
How to Train Your Dragon (film) 25, 47
Huck Finn 25, 41, 44, 54
Hudson, Henry 109, 111
Hughes, Langston 43
Hughes, Thomas 139
The Hunger Games (Collins) 42

I

identity
   individual identity in The Lion King 66
   in Tarzan Stories 91, 94, 97
   national identity 84, 92
   quest for identity in Peter Pan 44
   sensitivity readers and 112
   temptress females as lacking identity 28
imagery
   children's classics images, permanent stamp of 11
   loaded images in The Lion King 59
   male imagery in Tarzan stories 94
   Nazi imagery in Star Wars 75
   science fiction imagery in works of Butler 104
   villain as mirror image of the hero 23, 169
   visual images, sensory aspect of 33
   war imagery in children's stories 48
in Binti narrative 99
inciting incident 39
Independence Day (film) 168
Inglis-Arkell, Esther 132
Ishiguro, Kazuo 117
Island of the Blue Dolphins (O'Dell) 25, 53
Iyer, Nalini 55

J

James Bond 91
Jedi knights 70, 73–74, 185
The Joker 23, 130, 133, 168, 170
The Jungle Book (Kipling)
   as a Children's Classic 11

as problematic 117
film version 66, 67
in the Golden Age of children's literature 137
man vs. nature theme 179
Mowgli, character in 26, 41, 44, 51, 54
racism in 67
ruling class in 42
Seeds-of-Empire literature, as exemplifying 54

K

Katniss Everdeen 42, 165
Kaysen, Susanna 12
Kelen, Christopher 70
Kerslake, Patricia 82
Khair, Tabish 82
Kidnapped (Stevenson) 11, 24, 138
Kim, Myungsung 100
King Leopold of Belgium 79
King, Stephen 23, 43, 168
Kipling, Rudyard 11, 51, 54, 84, 117
Kozak, Anna 90, 92, 93–97
Kung Fu Panda (film) 25, 26

L

LaCapra, Dominick 43
Lagji, Amanda 98, 99, 102–107
Landis, Max 35
language and dialogue 9, 32, 36, 91, 99, 106, 149
Le Carre, John 33
Lee, Harper 112
Les Miserables (Hugo) 169
Lex Luthor 23, 169
LGBTQ portrayals 37, 152
The Lion King (film) 53, 59–68, 178
Little House on the Prairie (Wilder) 52, 70, 144
Little Orphan Annie 12, 26
The Little Prince (Saint-Exupery) 12, 55, 145
Lonetree, Amy 105
A Long Way Home (Brierley) 21
Lord of the Flies (Golding) 24, 53, 60, 69
Lord of the Rings (Tolkien) 13, 47, 50, 99, 173
Lubar, Steven 104
Lucas, George 32, 70, 73, 75–76, 78

M

Mackenzie, John 84, 85
Macron, Emmanuel 104
manic pixie dream girl character 35
masked fiction 55, 187
Mattson, Christina Phillips 148
Maxwell, Alexander 69, 70, 73–78

McCraney, Tarrell Alvin 116
Misemer, Leah 88
Mitchell, Lucy Sprague 34
Miyazaki, Hayao 67
Moby Dick (Melville) 168
Moore, Anne Carroll 35
Morgenstern, Karl 19
Mountfort, Paul 80, 86
Mufasa 59, 61, 64, 65
Munkittrick, Kyle 127, 128

N

"The Nation in Children's Literature" (Kelen/Sundmark) 70
Nazi
  Nazis as Hollywood villains 23, 75, 169
N.C. Wyeth illustrations 11, 22
Neely, Brett 73
Nervous Conditions (Dangarembga) 102
Ngũgĩ wa Thiong'o 106
Nick Fury 49
9/11 terrorist attacks 43, 49, 187
Nixon, Richard 70, 76
Nolen, William 71

O

obstacles 39, 44
October Sky (Hickam) 21, 25
Of Mice and Men (Steinbeck) 29
Okorafor, Nnedi 15, 98–101, 102, 103, 106
The Once and Future King (White) 24, 27
Oppenheimer, J. Robert 50
Orientalism 52, 81, 84, 86, 88, 110
orphaned-girl stories 35
Orwell, George 54, 60
Osborn, Norman 135
Osnos, Evan 26

P

Paste-Pot Pete 135
Peter Pan (Barrie) 11, 24, 137, 138, 141
Peter Parker 131, 169
Peter Rabbit (Potter) 11, 35, 137
Pixar 13, 63, 120–123, 123–125, 127–128
Plato on the Theory of Being 135
plot 30, 39, 40, 46, 74, 139
Pollyanna (Porter) 12, 35
Professor Snape 49, 139, 141, 145, 146, 170
Prose, Francine 112
Pullman, Phillip 44, 108–111, 115, 116, 119

Q

Queer theory 37
Questing Feminism (Wickham) 100
Quinby, Lee 168

R

Rank, Otto 19, 143
The Red Badge of Courage (Crane) 25, 54
Red Skull 23, 169
Rich, Adrienne 43
Richardson, Nick 135
Rick and Morty (animated series) 76, 77
rising action 39
Robbins, Jerome 32
Robinson Crusoe (Defoe) 53
Robocop (film) 23, 169
Roosevelt, Franklin 168
Roosevelt, Teddy 92, 95
Rousseau, Jean-Jaques 95
Rowling, J.K. 14, 36, 60, 77, 138–147
Rushdie, Salman 98
Russell, Danielle 27

S

Sadako and the Thousand Paper Cranes (Coerr) 12, 33, 48
Said, Edward 52, 55, 80–81, 84, 110, 116
Sandler, Adam 95
Sandman 131, 135, 170
Saving Private Ryan (film) 46, 47
Schilling, Dave 91
Scott, Ridley 78
Scrooge McDuck 41, 130
sensitivity readers 110, 112
setting 31, 44, 99, 106, 141
Shere Khan 51, 67
Sherlock Holmes character and films 46, 117, 146, 165
Shields, R.L. 108–111, 112–119
Short, Kathy G. 151
sidekicks 20, 22, 35, 99, 166
Silver Surfer 130, 131, 132
Simba 59–66
Slater, Dashka 16
slavery 43, 54, 103, 187
Sleeping Beauty 41, 121
Smith, Dinitia 37
Smith, Zadie 110, 117
Snow White 10, 41, 121
social Darwinism 59, 65
Socrates 129, 135
Spiderman films 23, 131, 168
Spielberg, Steven 46
Stanley, Henry 79
Star Wars films
   as a coming-of-age story 21, 25
   central theme 32
   character, importance of 31
   Darth Vader, character of 50, 170, 185
   influence on Harry Potter 143
   Luke Skywalker, as a character of 23, 169, 185
   masked version of war in 48
   political aspects of narrative 69–78
Steamboat Willie (film) 13
Steinbeck, John 29, 44
Summitt, Pat 182
Sundmark, Bjorn 70
Superman character and films 27, 131, 136, 164, 173
symmetry 30

T

Tal, Kali 43
Tannen, Deborah 36, 192–194
Tarzan stories
   caste system made clear in 54
   colonialism, associated with 94, 130
   ideal natural man, Tarzan portrayed as 95
   Lord Greystoke as true identity of Tarzan 91, 94
   nature as a narrative presence in 44
Terminator (films) 23, 168
The Color Purple (Walker) 24, 27, 187
The Comedian 130, 133
The Dark Fantastic (Thomas) 100
The Flash 130, 135
The Hobbit (Tolkien) 13, 21, 50, 137, 138
The Incredibles (film) 123–125
the Innocent 20, 22
theme
   beauty as a dominant theme in fairy tales 121
   Binti, African themes in 99
   Butler, mature themes in the works of 103
   children's literature, popular themes in 26, 41, 43
   in Fiddler on the Roof 32
   in Pixar rules 125
   man vs. nature theme, prose examples of 178
   masked fiction, imperial themes in 55
   poetry, identity as a theme in 27
the noble savage 22, 92
the Other 26–29, 79–83
The Punisher 31, 131
The Purge films 42
the setup 38–39
The Shining (King) 23, 168
The Strenuous Life (Roosevelt, T.) 92

Thomas, Ebony Elizabeth 100
Thor 130, 135
Thrasymachus 135
three-act model 38–40, 46, 182
Tintin adventures
   American readers, lack of interest in 88
   colonialism, associated with 87, 130
   European narrative, as part of 54, 79
   film versions 79
   imperialist sentiments of 80, 84–85
Tintin in Amerique 79
Tintin in the Congo 79
To Kill a Mockingbird (Lee) 9, 24
Tolkien, J.R.R. 13, 15, 31, 44, 50, 99, 138, 139
Torrance, Jack 23, 168
Toy Story films 121, 127
trauma 41, 187
Treasure Island (Stevenson) 11, 22, 24, 35, 138
Tripods series 110, 113
Twain, Mark 112, 113
Twilight series 24, 25, 42, 50, 71, 173

U

Us (film) 42

V

Vietnam War
   details of the war, keeping from the public 93
   just war status, not qualifying for 132
   movies, retelling the story of 187
   Star Wars, writing of inspired by 70, 76
   trauma stories and 43
villains
   as mirror image of heroes 23, 169
   British accent in majority of villains 42
   Clayton as a villain in Tarzan stories 92, 93
   essay questions on 167
   Human-as-Villain option in Pixar films 127
   in coming-of-age stories 20
   in Harry Potter stories 23, 60, 168, 170
   in Marvel comics 49, 135
   in Tintin stories 86
   invisibility as a superpower for the villain inside us 134
   motivation of 23, 131
   of the modern world 97
   Open Letter to a Villain assignment 174
   Paste-Pot Pete as a Kirby villain 135
   people of color, implied villainy of 100
   villainy, speculation on 167
Voldemort 60, 143, 144

W

Walker, Alice 187
Walker, Emma 79–89
Wall-E 121
Walzer, Michael 132
war and conflict
   cyber war, Ultron as personification of 49
   enemies, Otherizing during wartime 29
   High Empire war stories 54
   in children's picture books 149
   in literature of trauma 187
   in The Jungle Book 51
   "just war" theory 132
   Lord of the Rings, parallel with WWI 50
   masked version of war in young adult novels 48
War of the Worlds (film) 23, 168
Watchmen (print and film) 43, 100, 130, 133
White House Down (film) 23, 168
Why Should Superheroes Be Good? (Evans) 131
Wickham, Kimberly 100
Wilder, Billy 45–47
Wilder, Laura Ingalls 12, 44
Willy Wonka and the Chocolate Factory (film) 42, 60
The Wind in the Willows (Grahame) 11, 50, 52, 54, 137, 144

Y

Yabroff, Jennie 34
Younger, Brett 134

Z

Zeffirelli, Franco 47
Zizeck, Slavoj 42
zombies 28, 42, 114
Zootopia 67

Tom's Bio

Tom Durwood is a teacher, writer and editor with an interest in history. Tom most recently taught English Composition and Empire and Literature at Valley Forge Military College, where he won the Teacher of the Year Award five times. Tom has taught Public Speaking and Basic Communications as guest lecturer for the Naval Special Warfare Development Group at the Dam's Neck Annex of the Naval War College.

Tom is editor and publisher of an online scholarly journal, Empire Studies Magazine (www.empirestudies.org). Peter Suber, Berkman Fellow at Harvard University, an advocate of the open access movement, praises *Empire Studies* as "a new opportunity for overcoming access barriers to knowledge and research." Dr. Julian Fisher of Scholarly Exchange has also applauded Tom's efforts. "Creating valuable academic content and then hiding it behind financial firewalls—the traditional scholarly publishing model—runs counter to the essence of scholarship, learning and sharing," according to Fisher. "To see Empire Studies breaking that mold is exciting." The magazine interviews with a diverse group of scholars, including Anne Knowles, Mark Bowden, Tabish Khair and Jane Tompkins, among many others, and currently posts over forty features

Tom's ebook *Empire and Literature* matches global works of film and fiction to specific quadrants of empire, finding surprising parallels. Literature, film, art and architecture are viewed against the rise and fall of empire. In a foreword to Empire and Literature, postcolonial scholar Dipesh Chakrabarty of the University of Chicago calls it "imaginative and innovative." Prof. Chakrabarty writes that "Durwood has given us a thought-provoking introduction to the humanities."

Tom's ambitious new historical fiction series has earned positive reviews from early readers. "This has all the makings of a wonderful literary property," writes Sherri Smith of Park Road Books. "It's like The *Da Vinci Code* meets *Kidnapped*."

Gina Glenn of Malaprop Bookstore offers, "It's a clever premise, to have teenaged heroes coming of age and changing history, aided by the mysterious Society of Navigators … I place the writing with Steve Berry, Bernard Cornwell, A J Hartley, and even a little Dan Brown."

Tom's newspaper column "Shelter" appeared in the North County Times for seven years. Tom earned a Masters in English Literature in San Diego, where he also served as Executive Director of San Diego Habitat for Humanity.

Tom's Teaching

A superb leader. He projects the values of Valley Forge Military College to cadets, parents, alumni and colleagues. He brings a new perspective from the work place to Valley Forge Military College. Integrity above reproach. He unhesitatingly speaks his mind.

> **Professor Durwood is an outstanding teacher and scholar**. He is the embodiment of Valley Forge Military College – dedicated, credentialed, experience – and absolutely true to our Military College Mission "to build leaders of character, for the future, for the community, for the nation, and the world. **A gifted teacher.**
>
> -- Academic Dean Michael Krause
Valley Forge Military College
>
> **Tom Durwood is the best English professor I have ever seen** in my thirty-two years teaching at Valley Forge Military College … No one spends more time and effort seeking ways to turn students into effective writers than Tom. He has lesson plans that map out new ways to appeal to students and to make writing concrete to their experiences as well as their individual needs.
>
> Pat Murray Ph.d
Valley Forge Military College

Tom has a gift for making complex ideas understandable to his cadets. His lesson plans are amazing! He can turn a standard freshman composition class into a forum for collaborative learning and global thinking.

-- Susan Ray Ph.d
Valley Forge Military College

Credits

Artwork

Cover art Copyright @ 2020 by Zelda Devon. Original commission for "Kid Lit: An Introduction to Literary Criticism."

Artwork pages 139, 163, 182, 185, 191, and 192 copyright @ 2020 Kateryna Rybalka. Original commissions for "Kid Lit: An Introduction to Literary Criticism."

Artwork pages 67, 183, and 185 copyright @ 2020 Chau Matser. Original commissions for "Kid Lit: An Introduction to Literary Criticism."

Title page: Maxfield Parrish, 'Arabian Nights' (1909)

Page 9: Peter Rabbit, by Beatrix Potter (1907)

Page 11: N. C. Wyeth mural detail (1919)

Page 14: Tarzan's First Appearance in October, 1912, All-Story Magazine.

Page 16: 'Manga girl eyes in vector style.' Wikimedia Commons. Author: Sandra Hofer.

Page 17: Edmund Dulac's "The Snow Queen" (1911)

Page 22: N. C. Wyeth "Treasure Island" (1911)

Page 28: 'Assassins Creed' style helmeted warrior. Wikimedia Commons. Author: Iksokleb.

Page 30: Maxfield Parrish "The Lantern Bearers" (1908)

Page 38: Chart: Gabriel Moura, Elements of Cinema

Page 44: Arthur Rackham's "Alice" (1907)

Credits | 211

Page 45: Jesse Wilcox Smith, 'Reading on the Window Seat' from first edition, "A Child's Garden of Verses" (1896).

Page 52: Ernest Shephard, from "The Wind in the Willows."

Page 57: Maxfield Parrish, 'Arabian Nights' (1909)

Page 62: Rembrandt's portrayal of the Bible parable, "The Prodigal Son," which bears some similarity to "The Lion King" plot.

Page 65: Hamlet poster (1920) by Franz A. Peffer Poster for Hamlet. Asta Nielsen, Art-Film, Druck von Meissner & Buch.jpg.

Page 67: Compass by Chau Matser.

Page 69: "Cicero in the Roman Senate," a painting by Granger. The Roman Empire is a recurring civic model in modern science fiction.

Page 83: Milton Caniff's "Terry and the Pirates," another comic which plunged a Western protagonist into other cultures.

Page 85: Peter Pan is one of many children's classics with imperial roots. Art by Mabel Lucie Pullman (circa 1919)

Page 90: Frontispiece to "Tarzan of the Apes" (1914). Wikimedia Commons.

Page 92: Bookplate of Edgar Rice Burroughs.

Page 101: First edition of Frank Baum's "Dorothy and the Wizard of Oz" (1908). Wikimedia Commons.

Page 108: Explorer Robert McClure's The Investigator was trapped in ice throughout 1852. Authors like Phillip Pullman often use real-life episodes such as this one as the basis for his fiction.

Page 111: John Collier's painting of the arctic explorer Henry Hudson, his son, and loyal crew set adrift.

Page 117: Benjamin Jean Joseph Constant's "Arabian Nights" (circa 1899). An example of Orientalist art, a romanticized view of the East through Western eyes.

Page 129: Portrait of the rationalist Baruch Spinoza (artist unknown, circa 1665). Wikimedia Commons. Owlgirl, a little-know superheroine. Wikimedia Commons.

Page 132: Captain Battle, an obscure superhero. Wikimedia Commons.

Page 139: Moon and Clouds by Kateryna Rybalka.

Page 148: Little Red Riding Hood. Works Progress Administration poster by Kenneth Whitley, 1939. Wikimedia Commons.

Page 150: From "Dino Math: Sidd's Birthday," a storybook that teaches math. Empire Studies Press

Page 153: From "The Illustrated Boatman's Daughter." Art: Serena Malyon

Page 158: (Collage) "The Bibliophile" by Howard Pyle (1902). "The Young King of the Black Isles," painting by Maxfield Parrish (1906)

Page 163: Compass by Kateryna Rybalka.

Page 171: "David Killing Goliath" painting by Pietro da Cortona (1596–1669)

Page 172: Cover "A Princess of Mars" (1917) by Frank E. Schoonover.

Page 174: Sherlock Holmes poster. Wikimedia Commons. Author: Goldwyn Pictures.

Page 178: Jungle Boy by Chau Matser.

Page 182: Whale by Kateryna Rybalka.

Page 183: African figure with Machines by Chau Matser.

Page 185: Fox by Kateryna Rybalka.

Page 191: Sailboat by Kateryna Rybalka.

Page 192: Japanese girl by Kateryna Rybalka.

Photos

Page 7: Eskimo boy 1905 photo by Frank H. Nowell.

Page 19: Russian Hindu girl. Wikimedia Commons. Author: Rim sim.

Page 26: Hawaiian schoolchildren. Photo: Henry Wetherbee Henshaw (ca 1905)

Page 34: Comanche youth. Wikimedia Commons.

Page 41: Pashtun girl. Wikimedia Commons. Author: Senior Airman Bethann Hunt, Defenselink.

Page 48: Firefighters putting out a blaze in London after an air raid during the Blitz in 1941, an image recurring in such Kid Lit as 'Harry Potter.' Photo: National Archives, from the New York Times Paris Bureau Collection.

Page 49: Nagasaki atomic bomb mushroom cloud. Photo: Photo: Charles Levy, taken from one of the B-29 Superfortresses used in the attack. Office of War Information via Wikimedia Commons.

Page 59: Lion Cub. Wikimedia Commons. Photo: Vinodtiwari2608.

Page 71: Leaders MLK and LBJ in White House. Debate raged over the Vietnam War. Photo: National Archives

Page 75: U.S. soldiers in the Vietnam War Wikimedia Commons. Privates First Class Carl Baden (New Orleans, Louisiana) and Arcadio Carrion (Puerto Rico) of Company B, 3rd Battalion, 47th Infantry, 9th Infantry Division, laying in the mud waiting for artillery to knock out the 50 Cal. machine gun bunker that has them pinned down in a tree line at My Tho. Photo: SP4 Dennis J. Kurpius, 221st Signal Company (Pic)

Page 79: The explorer Henry Stanley posing later (in London) with Kalulu in the "suit he wore" when he found Livingstone in central Africa (1874).

Credits | 215

Page 81 : The Herge Museum opened in 2009 in Louvain-la-Neuve, Belgium. Creative Commons English Wikipedia. Photo: Peripatetic

Page 97: Elmo Lincoln as Tarzan (1918). Pretty Clever films.

Page 98: Nigerian statuettes, Musee de Quai Branly. Wikimedia Commons Author: Siren-Com.

Page 103: Octavia Butler, pioneer author of 'Afrofuturism,' at a book signing. Wikimedia Commons.

Page 105: The Sun Ra Arkestra performing in London in 2010. Wikimedia Commons. Author: Andy Newcombe.

Page 107: Natural History Museum of London. Wikimedia Commons. Photo: jhlau – a canvas of light.

Page 115: Polar bear swimming. Wikimedia Commons. Photo: John.

Page 119: Pope Francis. Wikimedia Commons. Photo: Jeffrey Bruno.

Page 120: Clown fish in the Andaman Coral Reef. Wikimedia Commons. Author: Ritiks.

Page 124: Pixar lamp. Wikimedia Commons. Mostra Pixar al PAC (Padiglione d'Arte Contemporanea) di Milano. Author: Pava

Page 128: Balloon festival of Albuquerque. Wikimedia Commons. Author: Eric Ward

Page 133: The philosopher Jean-Paul Sartre. Wikimedia Commons. Photo: Moshe Milner

Page 137: A troll statue at the Atu Vanska park. Credit: Wikimedia Commons.

Page 142: Kenilworth Castle, England. Wikimedia Commons. Photo: Tilliebean

Page 145: Codebreaking in WWII Wikimedia Commons

Page 156: Carlisle Indian Industrial School, PA (c. 1900). Photo credit: Wikimedia Commons. Once under-represented, groups like Native Americans today tell their own stories., public domain.

Page 158: (collage) Pashtun girl. Wikimedia Commons. Author: Senior Airman Bethann Hunt, Defenselink. Clown fish in the Andaman Coral Reef. Wikimedia Commons. Author: Ritiks.

Page 167: Wikimedia Commons. Batman villains The Penguin (Burgess Meredith), The Riddler (Frank Gorshin), and The Joker (Cesar Romero). Author: Greenway Productions.

Page 176: Wikimedia Commons. Osaka after the 1945 air raid. Unknown author - Japanese book "Showa History of 100 million people: Occupation of Japan Vol.2" published by Mainichi Newspapers Company.

Page 195: Bald eagle. Wikimedia Commons. Photo: Ra-smit.

www.ingramcontent.com/pod-product-compliance
Lightning Source LLC
Chambersburg PA
CBHW051352110526
44591CB00025B/2980